PIANO • VOCAL • GUITAR

W9-BJP-627

THE BEST CHRISTMAS SONGS EVER

ISBN 0-88188-928-8

HAL•LEONARD
CORPORATION

7777 W. BLUEMOUND RD. P.O. BOX 13819 MILWAUKEE, WI 53213

CONTENTS

THE BEST CHRISTMAS SONGS EVER

4	Angels From The Realms Of Glory
6	Angels We Have Heard On High
10	Auld Lang Syne
12	Away In A Manger (Luther/Spillman)
24	Away In A Manger (Mueller)
14	Blue Christmas
16	C-H-R-I-S-T-M-A-S
18	Chipmunk Song, The
20	Christ Was Born On Christmas Day
22	Christmas Waltz, The
27	Coventry Carol, The
28	Deck The Halls
30	Do They Know It's Christmas?
35	Feliz Navidad
38	First Noel, The
40	Frosty The Snow Man
44	God Rest Ye Merry, Gentlemen
43	Good Christian Men, Rejoice
46	Greatest Gift Of All, The
51	Happy Holiday
54	Happy Xmas (War Is Over)
58	Hard Candy Christmas
62	Hark! The Herald Angels Sing
64	He
66	Here We Come A-Wassailing
68	Holly Jolly Christmas, A
71	(There's No Place Like) Home For The Holidays
74	I Heard The Bells On Christmas Day
78	I Heard The Bells On Christmas Day (Traditional)
76	I Saw Mommy Kissing Santa Claus
79	I'll Be Home For Christmas
82	It Came Upon The Midnight Clear
85	It's Christmas In New York
90	Jingle Bells
92	Jingle-Bell Rock
95	Jolly Old St. Nicholas
96	Joy To The World

98 Last Month Of The Year, The
(What Month Was Jesus Born In?)

104 Let It Snow! Let It Snow! Let It Snow!

106 March Of The Toys

110 Marshmallow World, A

112 Most Wonderful Day Of The Year, The

101 My Favorite Things

116 Night Before Christmas Song, The

119 Nuttin' For Christmas

122 O Christmas Tree

124 O Come All Ye Faithful (Adeste Fidelis)

126 O Holy Night

123 O Little Town Of Bethlehem

130 Old Toy Trains

136 Once In Royal David's City

133 Parade Of The Wooden Soldiers

138 Pretty Paper

141 Rockin' Around The Christmas Tree

144 Rudolph The Red-Nosed Reindeer

147 Santa Baby

150 Santa, Bring My Baby Back (To Me)

156 Silent Night

158 Silver And Gold

153 Silver Bells

160 Star Carol, The

162 Suzy Snowflake

164 That Christmas Feeling

166 There Is No Christmas Like A
Home Christmas

161 Toyland

168 Twelve Days Of Christmas, The

170 Up On The Housetop

172 We Three Kings Of Orient Are

182 We Wish You A Merry Christmas

174 What Child Is This?

176 You Make It Feel Like Christmas

180 You're All I Want For Christmas

ANGELS FROM THE REALMS OF GLORY

Words by JAMES MONTGOMERY
Music by HENRY SMART

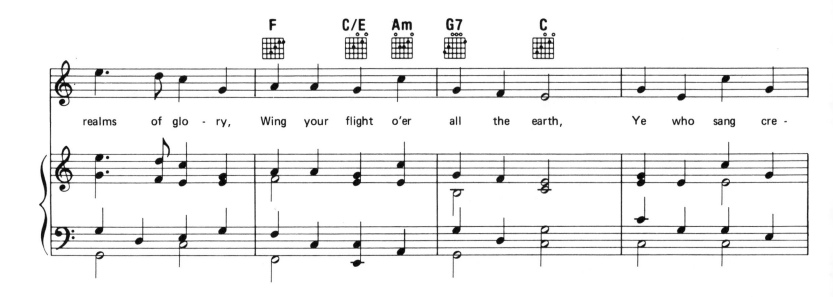

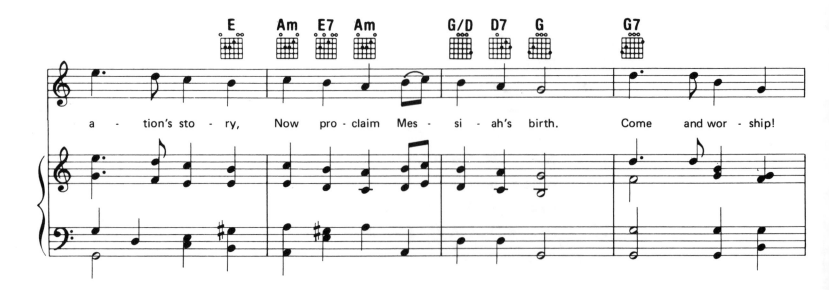

ANGELS WE HAVE HEARD ON HIGH

Moderately

French-English

AULD LANG SYNE

Words by ROBERT BURNS
Traditional Melody

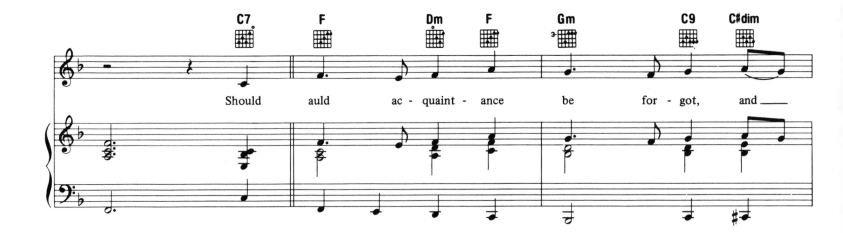

Should auld ac-quaint-ance be for-got, and ____

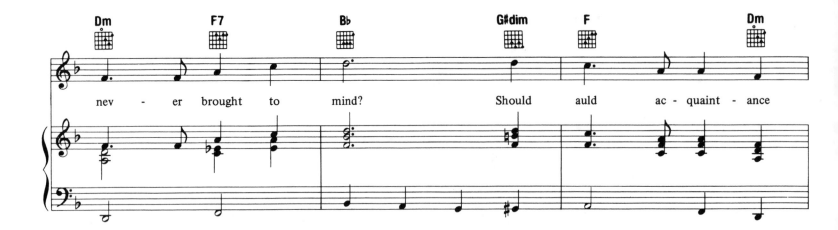

nev - er brought to mind? Should auld ac-quaint - ance

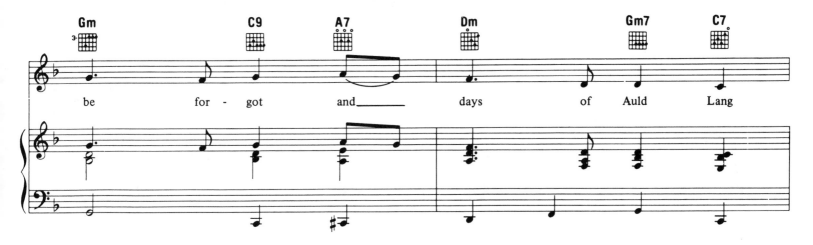

be for - got and_____ days of Auld Lang

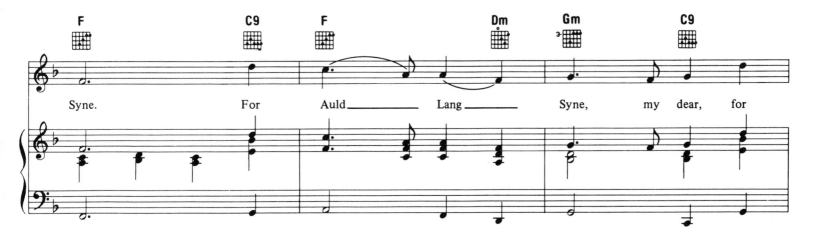

Syne. For Auld_____ Lang_____ Syne, my dear, for

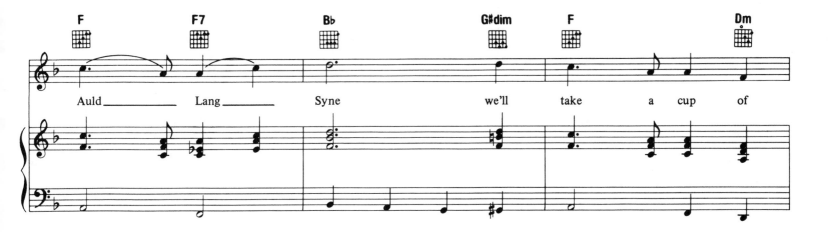

Auld_____ Lang_____ Syne we'll take a cup of

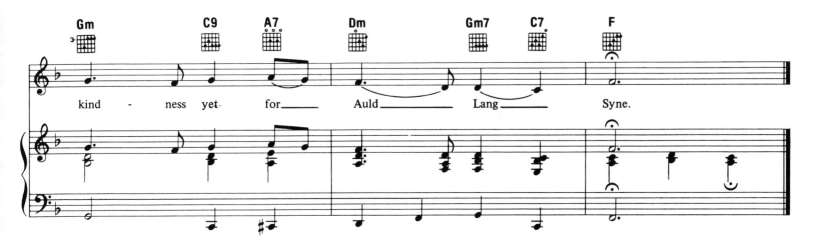

kind - ness yet for_____ Auld_____ Lang_____ Syne.

AWAY IN A MANGER

Words by MARTIN LUTHER
Music by JONATHAN E. SPILLMAN

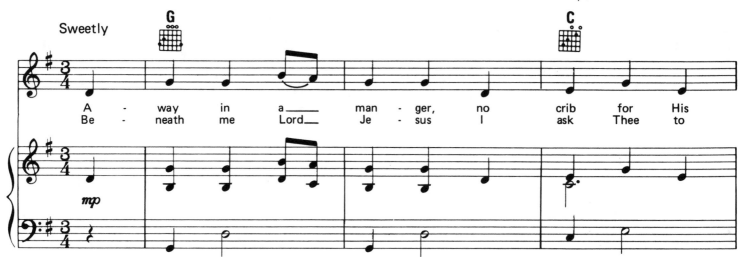

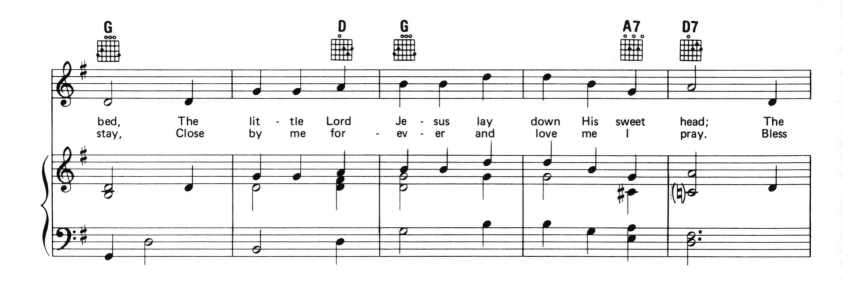

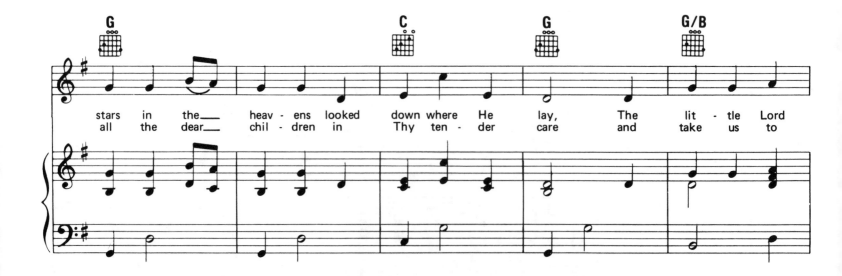

BLUE CHRISTMAS

Words and Music by
BILLY HAYES and JAY JOHNSON

Slowly

I'll have a

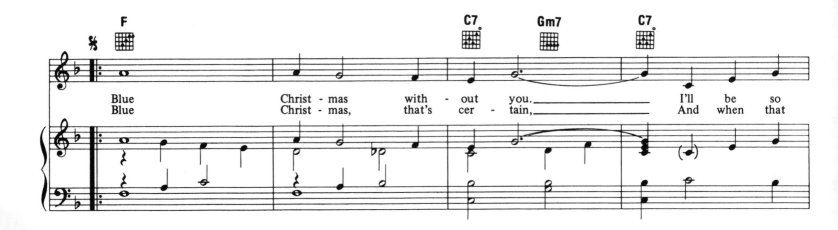

Blue Christ - mas with - out you._____ I'll be so
Blue Christ - mas, that's cer - tain,_____ And when that

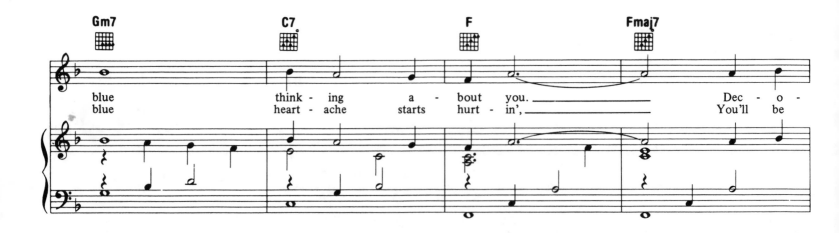

blue think - ing a - bout you._____ Dec - o -
blue heart - ache starts hurt - in',_____ You'll be

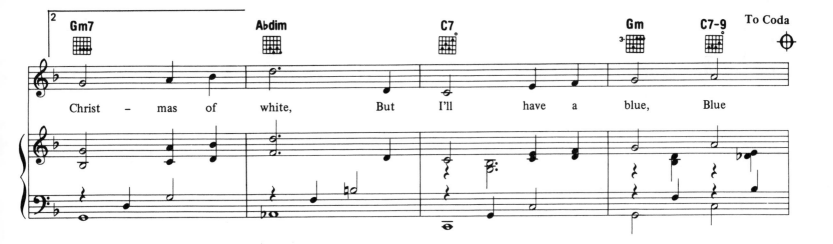

C-H-R-I-S-T-M-A-S

Moderato (with expression)

Words by JENNY LOU CARSON
Music by EDDY ARNOLD

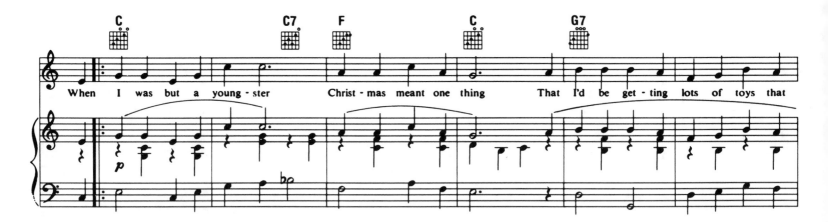

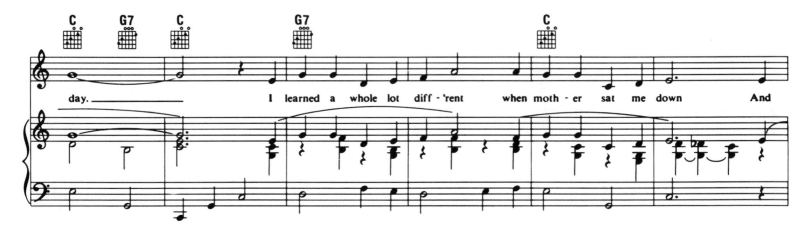

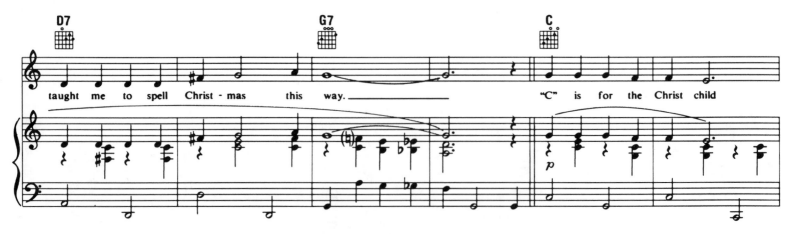

THE CHIPMUNK SONG

Words and Music by
ROSS BAGDASARIAN

CHRIST WAS BORN ON CHRISTMAS DAY

German

Lilting

mf

Christ was born on Christ - mas day,

Wreath the hol - ly, twine the bay;

Christ - us na - tus ho - di - e; The Babe, the Son, the

THE CHRISTMAS WALTZ

Words by SAMMY CAHN
Music by JULE STYNE

Moderately, with expression

Frost - ed win - dow panes,___ can - dles gleam - ing in - side, Paint - ed can - dy canes___

___ on the tree; San - ta's on his way, he's filled his

sleigh with things,_____ Things for you and for me. It's that time of year,

AWAY IN A MANGER

Words by MARTIN LUTHER
Music by CARL MUELLER

Sweetly

A -

way   in a   man - ger, no   crib   for a

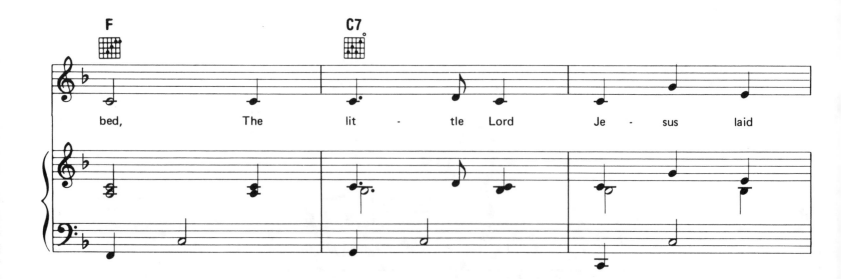

bed,   The   lit - tle Lord   Je - sus laid

THE COVENTRY CAROL

English, 16th Century

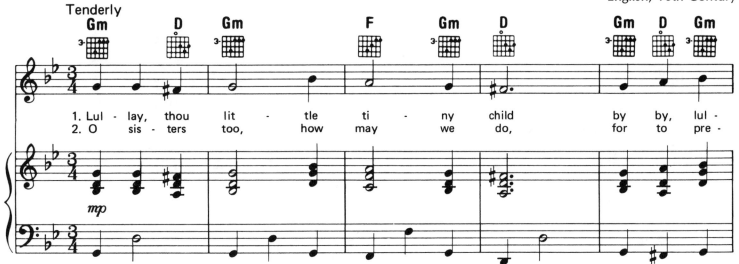

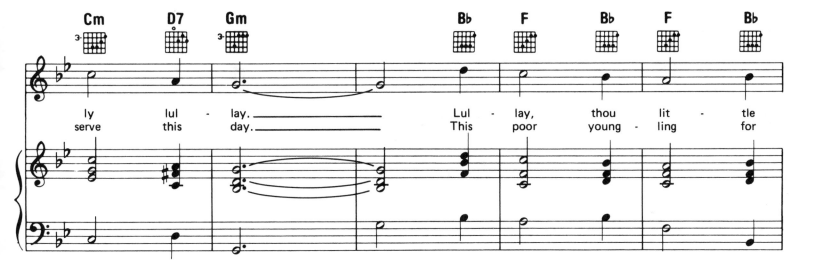

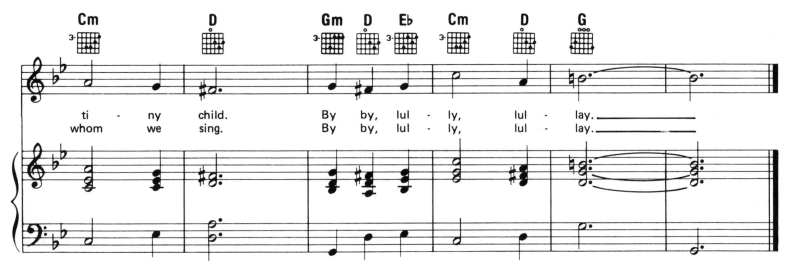

3. Herod the king,
   In his raging,
   Charged he hath this day.
   His men of might,
   In his own sight,
   All young children to slay.

4. That woe is me,
   Poor child for thee!
   And ever morn and day,
   For thy parting
   Neither say nor sing
   By by, lully lullay!

DECK THE HALLS

Welsh

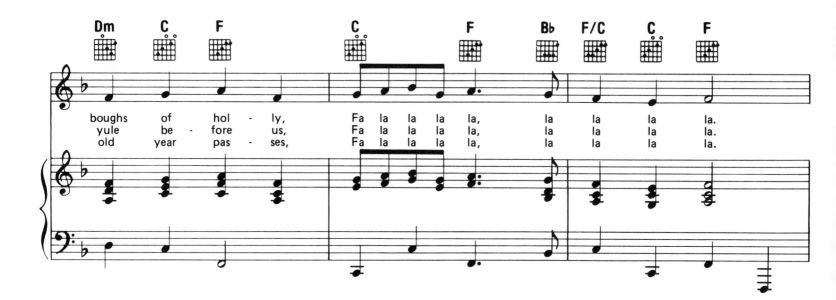

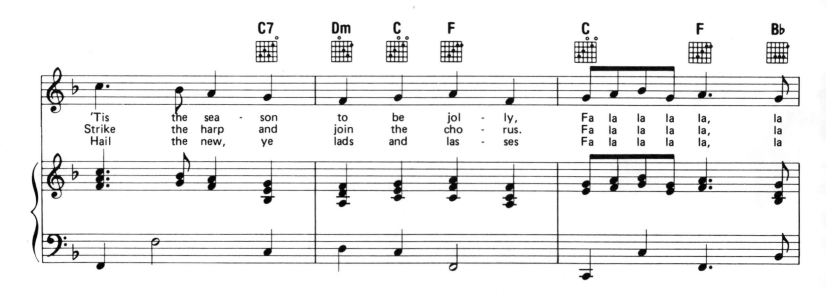

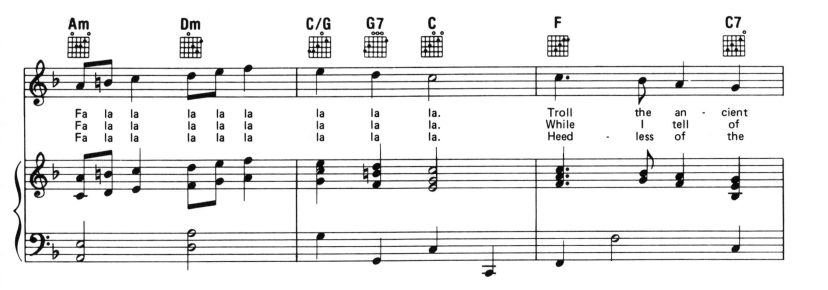

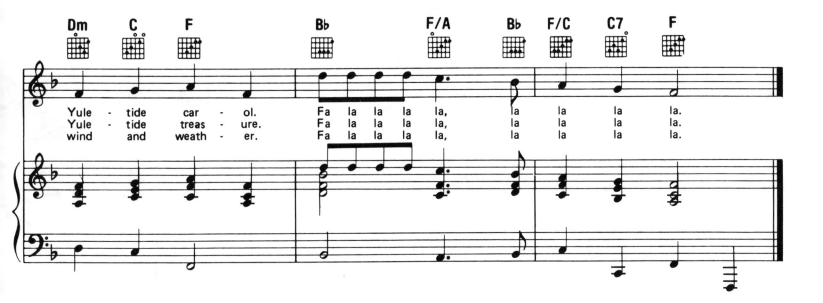

DO THEY KNOW IT'S CHRISTMAS?

Medium Rock

Words and Music by
M. URE and B. GELDOF

FELIZ NAVIDAD

Words and Music by
JOSE FELICIANO

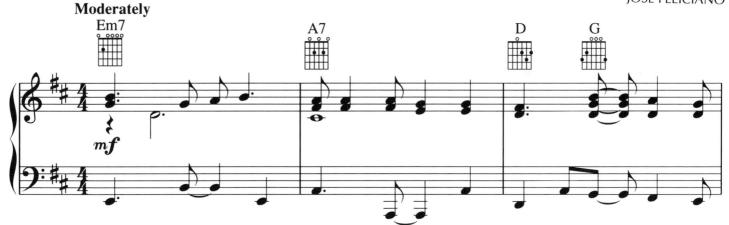

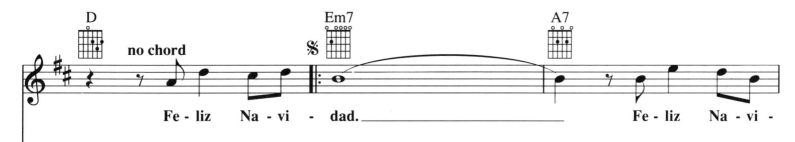

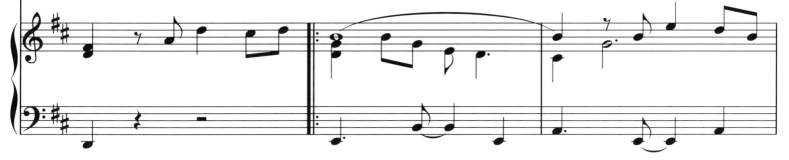

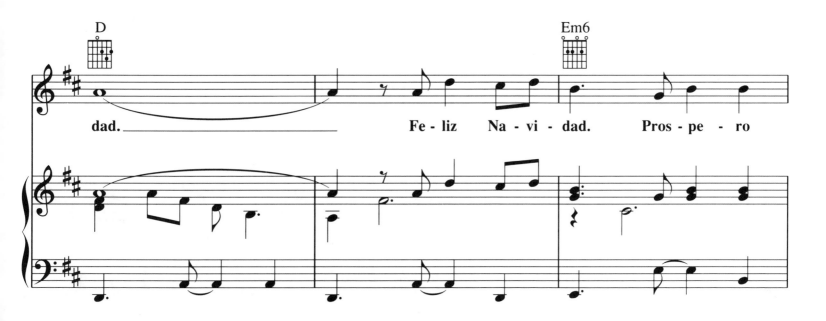

THE FIRST NOEL

French-English

Moderately slow

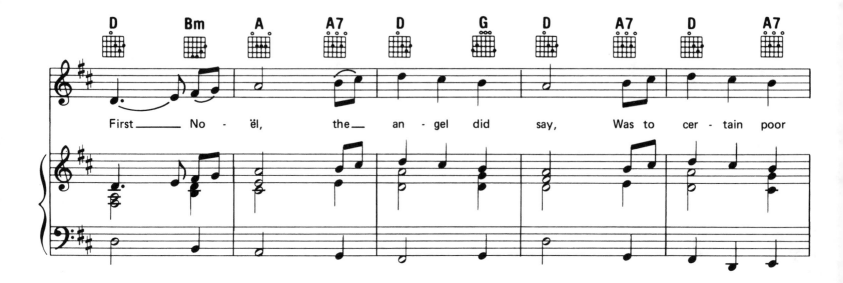

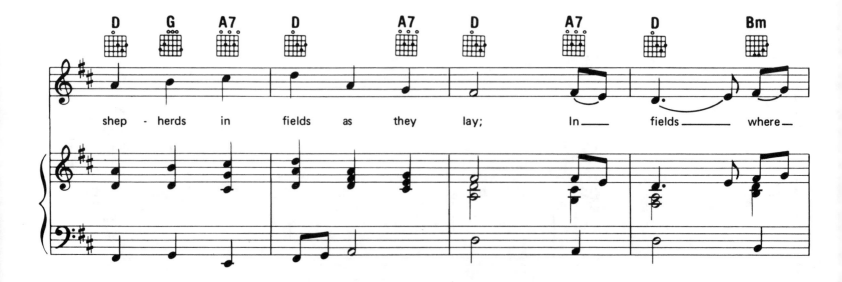

2. They looked up and saw a star
   Shining in the East, beyond them far;
   And to the earth it gave great light,
   And so it continued both day and night.

   Refrain

3. And by the light of that same star,
   Three wise men came from country far;
   To seek for a King was their intent,
   And to follow the star wherever it went.

   Refrain

4. This star drew night to the northwest,
   O'er Bethlehem it took its rest;
   And there it did both stop and stay,
   Right over the place where Jesus lay.

   Refrain

5. Then entered in those wise men three,
   Full reverently upon their knee;
   And offered there in His presence,
   Their gold, and myrrh, and frankincense.

   Refrain

FROSTY THE SNOW MAN

Words and Music by
STEVE NELSON and JACK ROLLINS

Moderato

1. FROS - TY, THE SNOW MAN was a jol - ly hap - py soul,___ With a
2. FROS - TY, THE SNOW MAN knew the sun was hot that day,___ So he

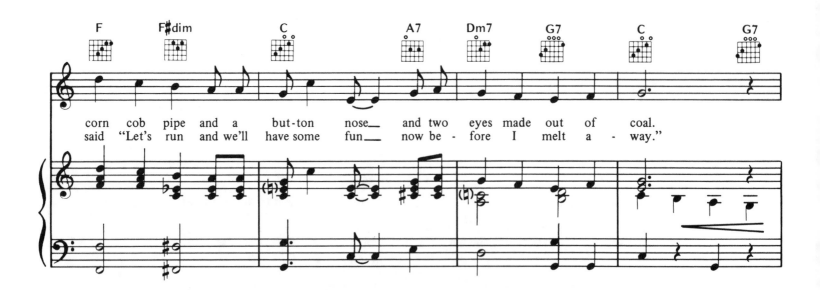

corn cob pipe and a but - ton nose___ and two eyes made out of coal.
said "Let's run and we'll have some fun___ now be - fore I melt a - way."

GOOD CHRISTIAN MEN, REJOICE

German, 14th Century
Words translated by JOHN M. NEALE

Good Chris-tian Men, Re - joice____ with heart and soul and voice,____ Give ye heed to
Good Chris-tian Men, Re - joice____ with heart and soul and voice,____ Now ye hear of

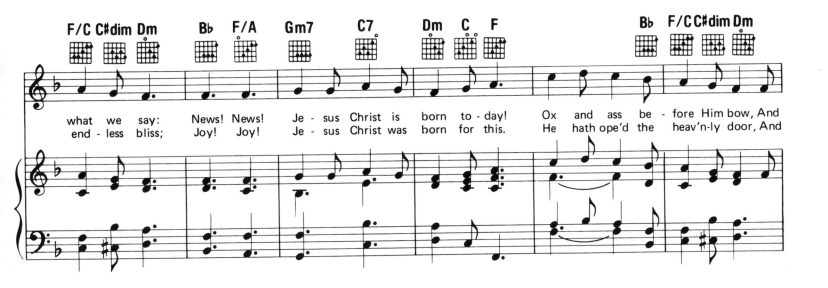

what we say: News! News! Je - sus Christ is born to - day! Ox and ass be - fore Him bow, And
end - less bliss; Joy! Joy! Je - sus Christ was born for this. He hath ope'd the heav'n-ly door, And

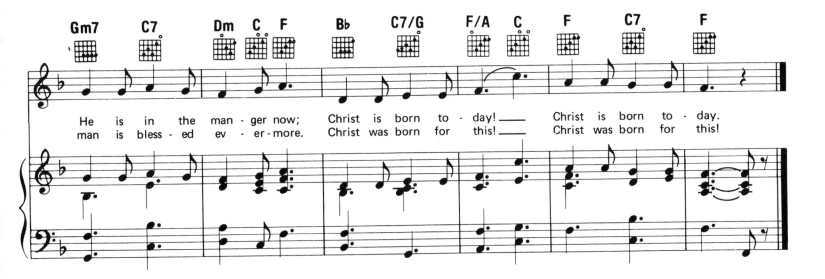

He is in the man - ger now; Christ is born to - day!____ Christ is born to - day.
man is bless - ed ev - er-more. Christ was born for this!____ Christ was born for this!

GOD REST YE MERRY, GENTELMEN

Moderately

English

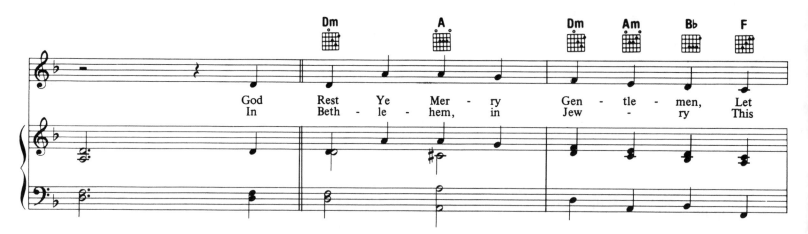

God   Rest   Ye   Mer - ry   Gen - tle - men,   Let
In   Beth - le - hem,   in   Jew - ry   This

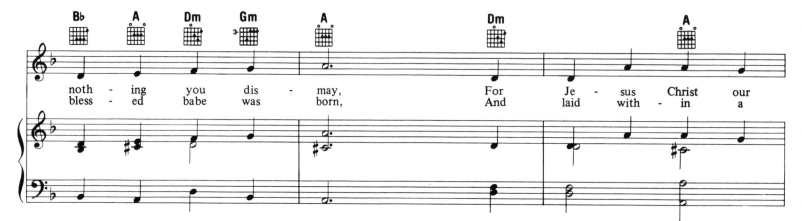

noth - ing   you   dis - may,   For   And   Je - sus   Christ   our
bless - ed   babe   was   born,   laid   with - in   a

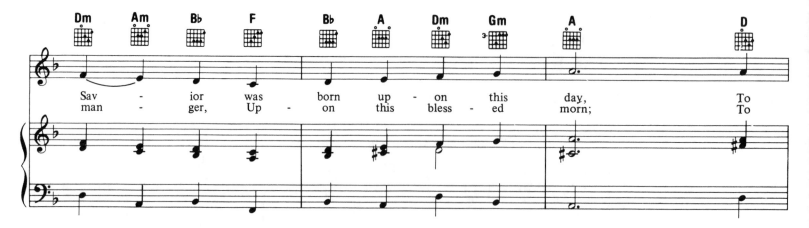

Sav - ior   was   born   up - on   this   day,   To
man - ger,   Up - on   this   bless - ed   morn;   To

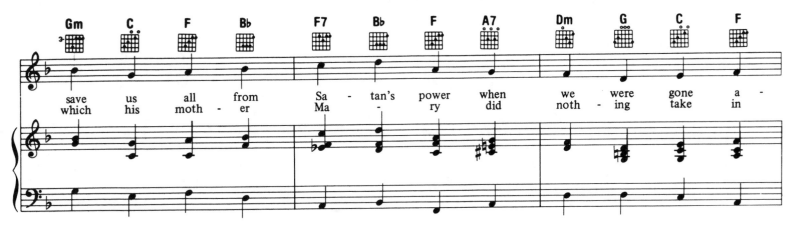

save us all from Sa - tan's power when we were gone a -
which his moth - er Ma - ry did noth - ing take in

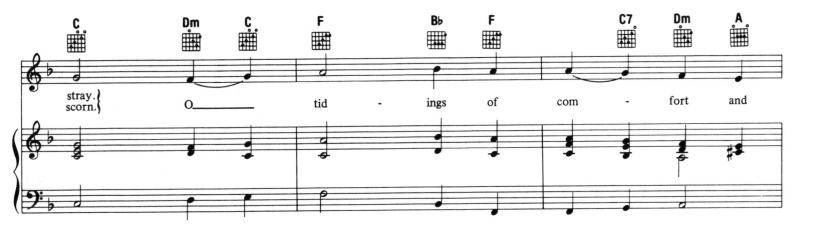

stray.
scorn.} O_____ tid - ings of com - fort and

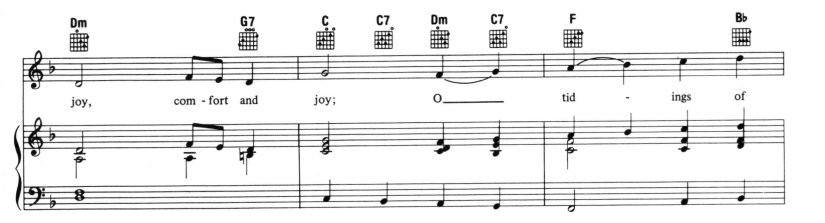

joy, com - fort and joy; O_____ tid - ings of

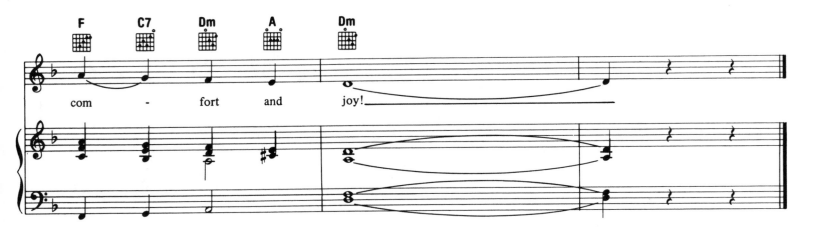

com - fort and joy!_____

THE GREATEST GIFT OF ALL

Words and Music by
JOHN JARVIS

for crea - tures great and small.   Peace on earth good___

will   to men   is the great - est gift of___ all.

Peace on earth good___ will   to men   is the great - est gift

of___ all.___

rit.

HAPPY HOLIDAY

(From The Motion Picture Irving Berlin's "HOLIDAY INN")

Words and Music by
IRVING BERLIN

hol - i - day, _____ hap - py hol - i - day. _____

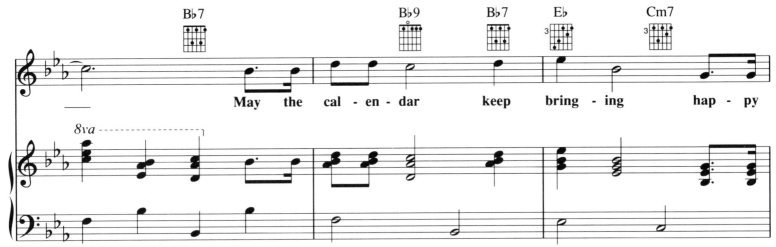

_____ May the cal - en - dar keep bring - ing hap - py

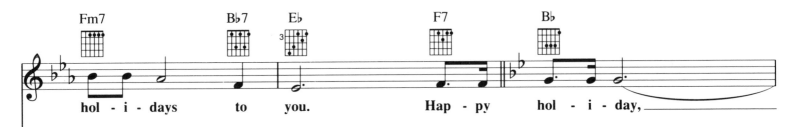

hol - i - days to you. Hap - py hol - i - day, _____

_____ hap - py hol - i - day. _____ While the

HAPPY XMAS (WAR IS OVER)

Words and Music by
JOHN LENNON and YOKO ONO

HARD CANDY CHRISTMAS

Words and Music by
CAROL HALL

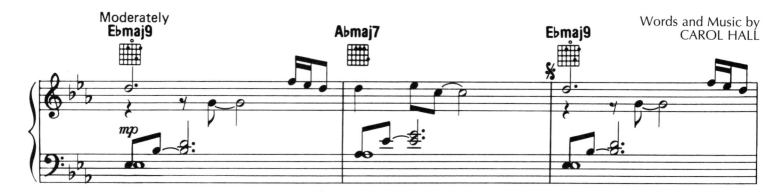

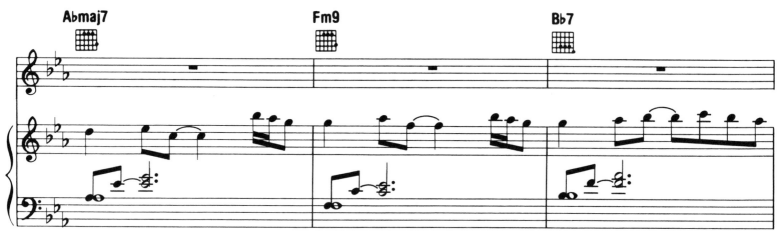

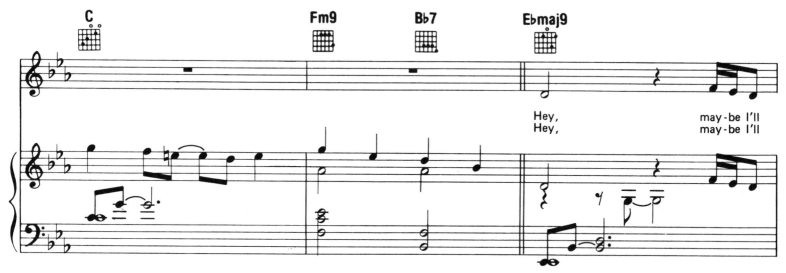

Hey,
Hey,
may-be I'll
may-be I'll

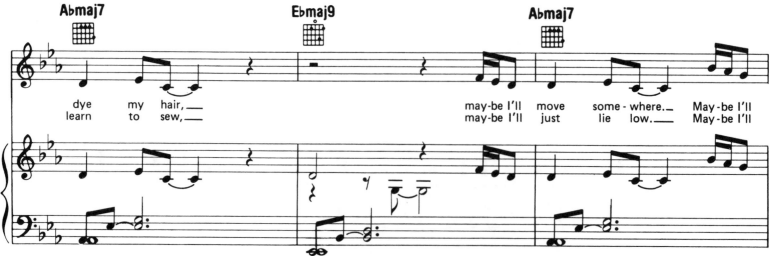

dye my hair, ___
learn to sew, ___

may-be I'll move some-where. ___ May-be I'll
may-be I'll just lie low. ___ May-be I'll

-dy. Lord, it's like a hard can - dy Christ-mas. I'm bare - ly get - ting

through to - mor - row, still I won't let sor - row bring me way down._

I'll be__ fine.

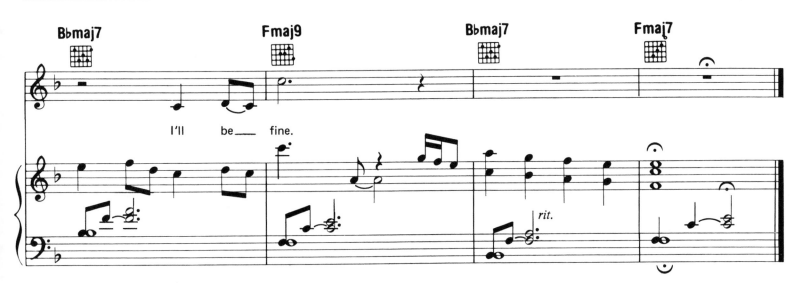

I'll be__ fine.

HARK! THE HERALD ANGELS SING

Words by CHARLES WESLEY
Music by FELIX MENDELSSOHN-BARTHOLDY

Joyfully

Hark! The Her - ald An - gels Sing,_____ "Glo - ry to the new - born King! Peace on earth, and

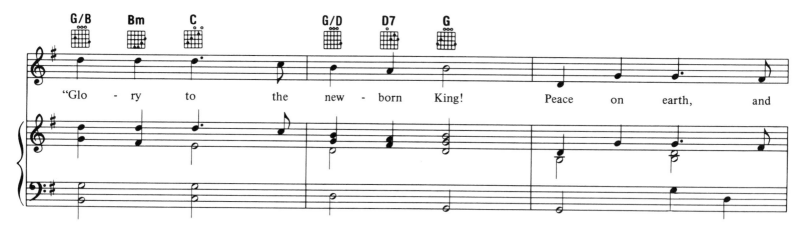

mer - cy mild,_____ God and sin - ners re - con - ciled."

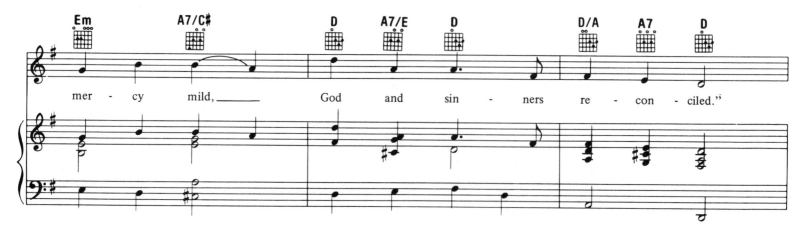

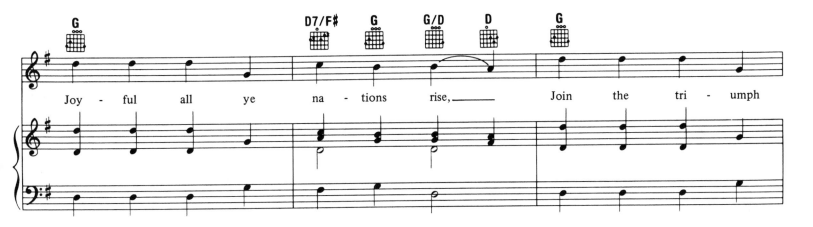

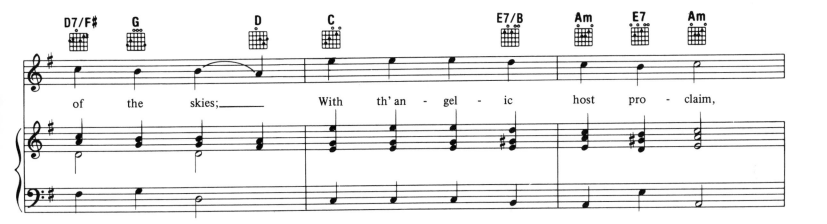

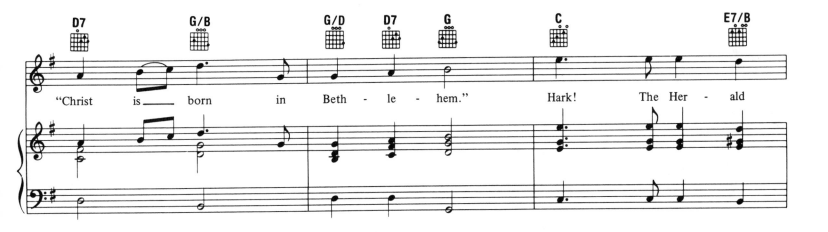

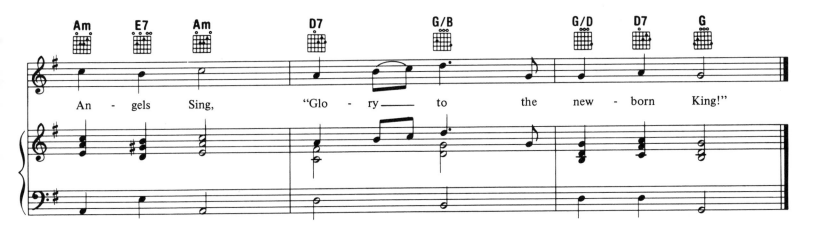

HE

Words by RICHARD MULLEN
Music by JACK RICHARDS

Moderately slow

He _____ can turn the tides _____ and calm the an — gry _____ sea.
He _____ can grant a wish _____ or make a dream come true.

He _____ a - lone de - cides _____ who writes a sym — pho — ny.
He _____ can paint the clouds _____ and turn the gray to blue.

He _____ lights ev - 'ry star _____ that makes our dark — ness bright.
He _____ a - lone knows where _____ to find the rain — bow's end.

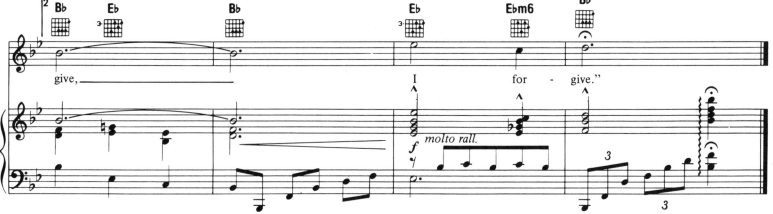

HERE WE COME A-WASSAILING

English

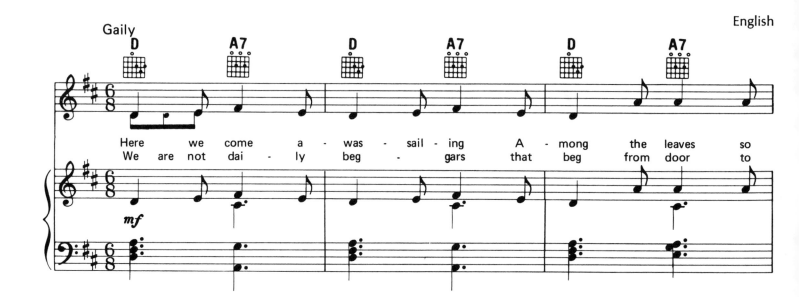

Here we come a-was-sail-ing A-mong the leaves so
We are not dai-ly beg-gars That beg from door so

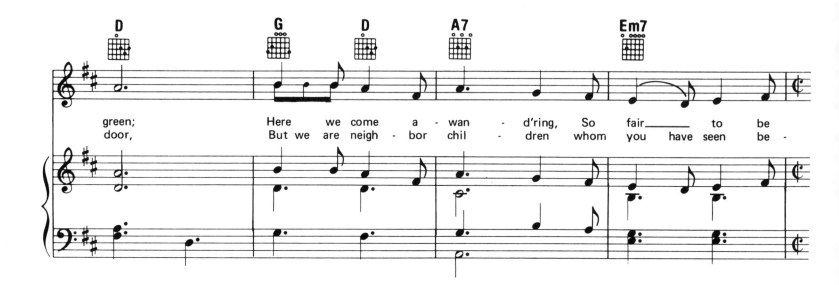

green; Here we come a-wan-d'ring, So fair_____ to be
door, But we are neigh-bor chil-dren whom you have seen be-

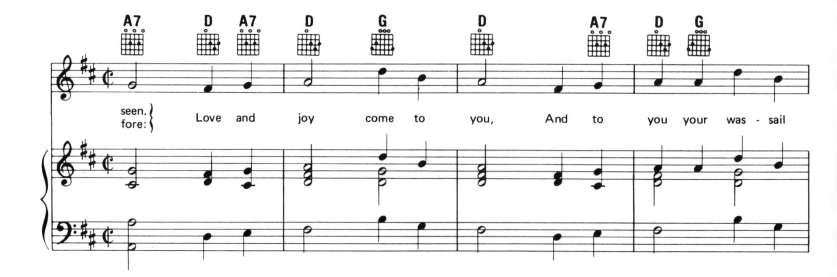

seen. } Love and joy come to you, And to you your was-sail
fore:

3. We have got a little purse
   Of stretching leather skin;
   We want a little money
   To line it well within:

4. God bless the master of this house,
   Likewise the mistress too;
   And all the little children
   That round the table go:

A HOLLY JOLLY CHRISTMAS

Music and Lyrics by
JOHNNY MARKS

Moderately bright with a happy feeling

Have A Hol - ly Jol - ly Christ - mas, it's the best time of the year.

I don't know if there'll be snow but

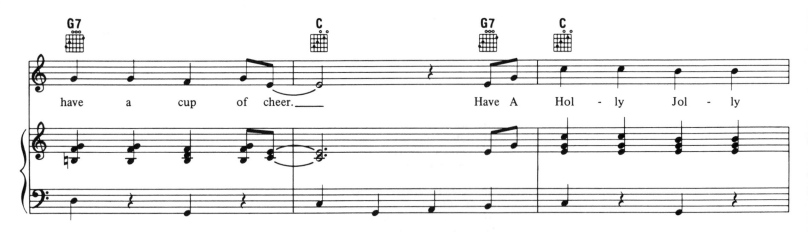

have a cup of cheer. Have A Hol - ly Jol - ly

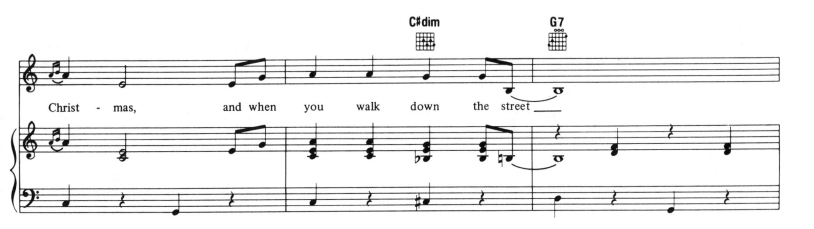

Christ - mas, and when you walk down the street ___

Say hel - lo to friends you know and ev - 'ry - one you

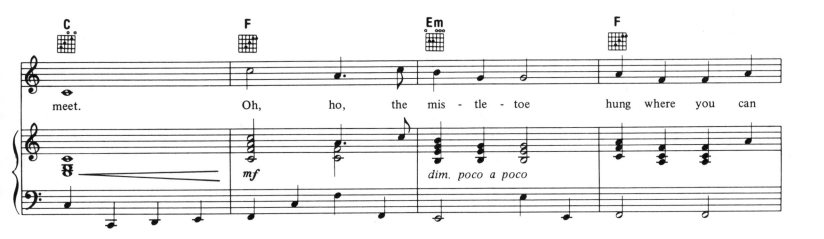

meet. Oh, ho, the mis - tle - toe hung where you can

see. Some - bod - y waits for you, kiss her once for

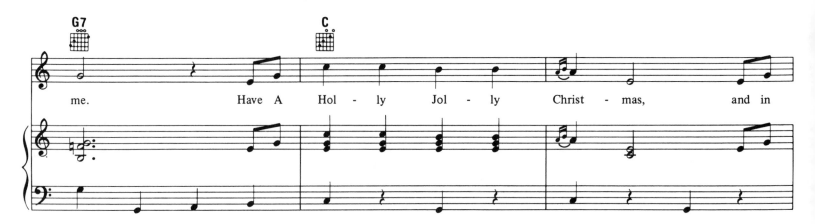

me. Have A Hol - ly Jol - ly Christ - mas, and in

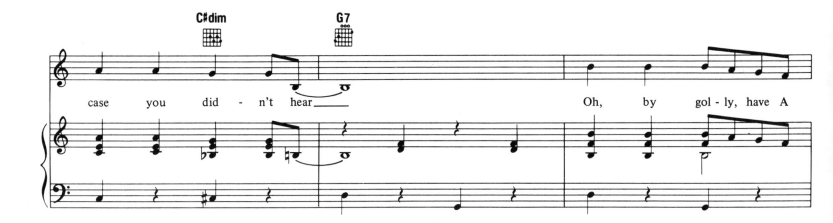

case you did - n't hear_____ Oh, by gol - ly, have A

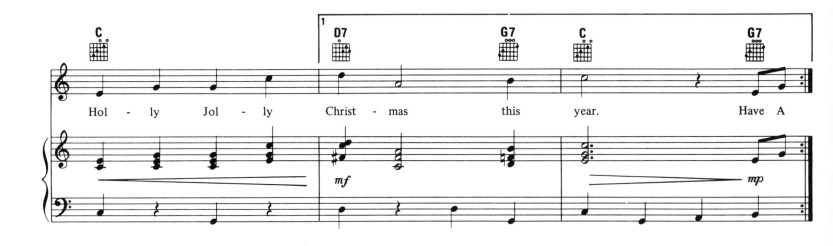

Hol - ly Jol - ly Christ - mas this year. Have A

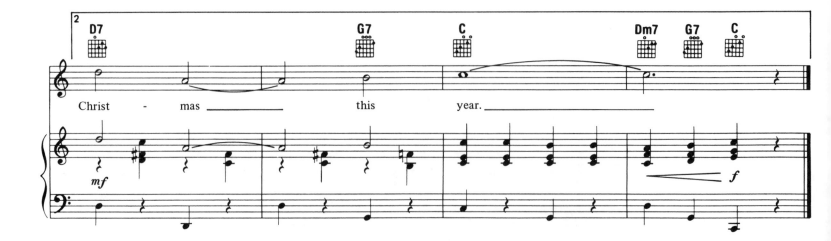

Christ - mas _____ this year. _____

(THERE'S NO PLACE LIKE)
HOME FOR THE HOLIDAYS

Words by AL STILLMAN
Music by ROBERT ALLEN

Moderato, With Feeling

Oh, there's no place like home for the hol-i-days_____ 'cause no mat-ter how far a-way you roam_____ When you pine for the sun-shine of a friend-ly gaze_____ for the hol-i-days you

I HEARD THE BELLS ON CHRISTMAS DAY

Words by HENRY LONGFELLOW
Adapted by JOHNNY MARKS
Music by JOHNNY MARKS

Moderately slow

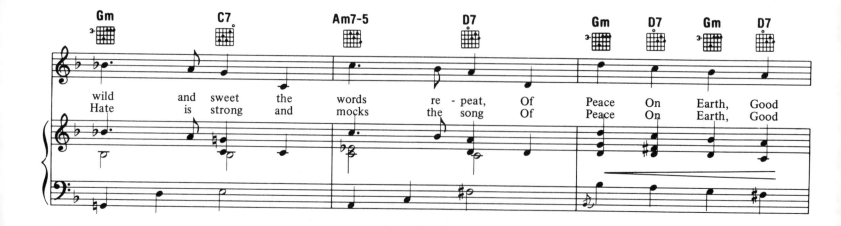

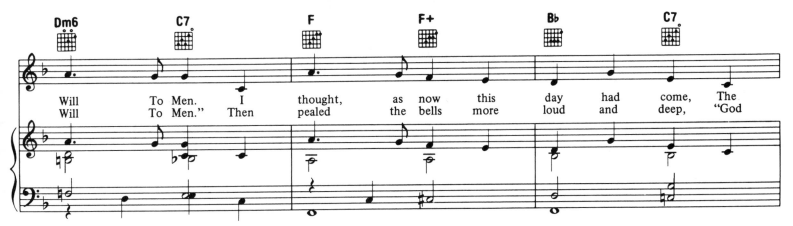

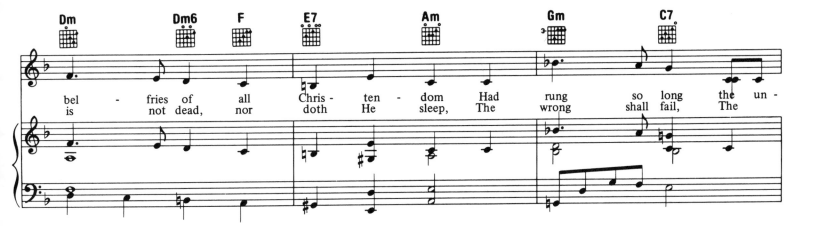

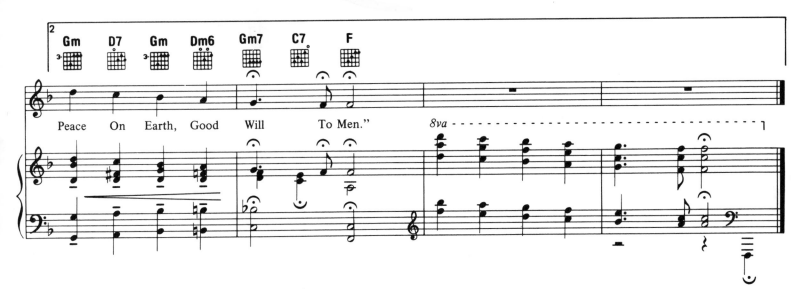

I SAW MOMMY KISSING SANTA CLAUS

Words and Music by
TOMMIE CONNOR

Moderately slow

I saw Mom-my kiss-ing San - ta Claus, un-der-neath the

mis-tle-toe last night. She did-n't see me creep down the

stairs to have a peep, she thought that I was tucked up in my bed-room fast a-

I HEARD THE BELLS ON CHRISTMAS DAY

Words by HENRY WADSWORTH LONGFELLOW
Music by JOHN BAPTISTE CALKIN

I heard the bells on Christ - mas day Their old fa - mil - iar
I thought how as on the day had come, The bel - fries of all

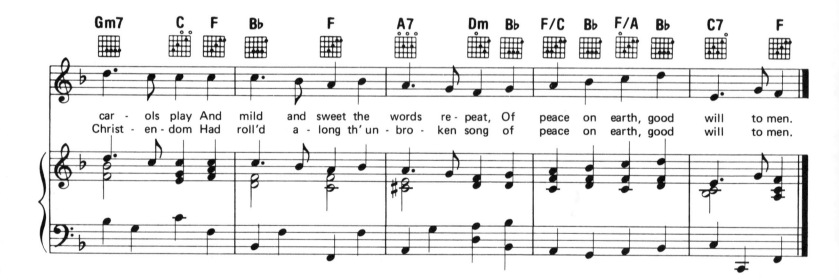

car - ols play And mild and sweet the words re - peat, Of peace on earth, good will to men.
Christ - en - dom Had roll'd a - long th' un - bro - ken song of peace on earth, good will to men.

3. And in despair I bow'd my head:
   "There is no peace on earth," I said,
   "For hate is strong, and mocks the song
   Of peace on earth, good will to men."

4. Then pealed the bells more loud and deep:
   "God is not dead, nor doth He sleep;
   The wrong shall fail, the right prevail,
   With peace on earth, good will to men."

5. Till, ringing, singing on its way,
   The world revolved from night to day,
   A voice, a chime, a chant sublime,
   Of peace on earth, good will to men!

I'LL BE HOME FOR CHRISTMAS

Words and Music by
KIM GANNON and WALTER KENT

Moderately slow

Verse

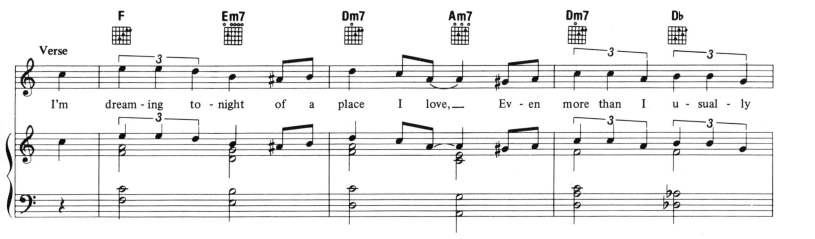

I'm dream-ing to-night of a place I love,___ Ev - en more than I u - sual - ly

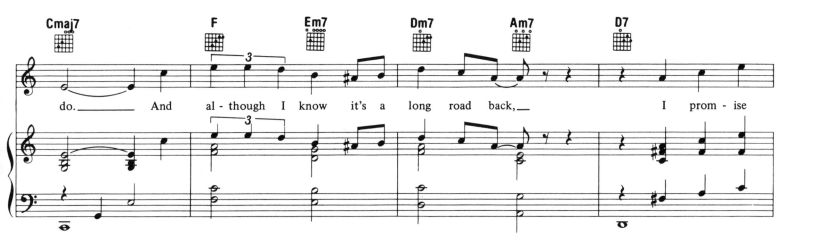

do._____ And al-though I know it's a long road back,___ I prom - ise

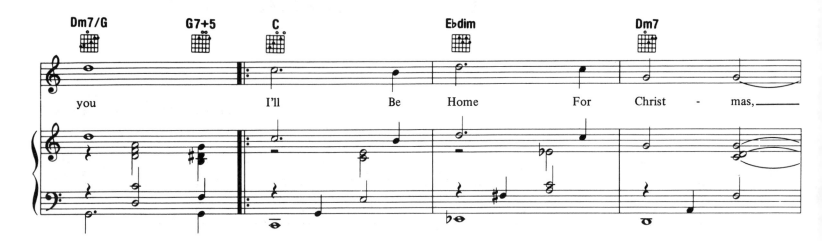

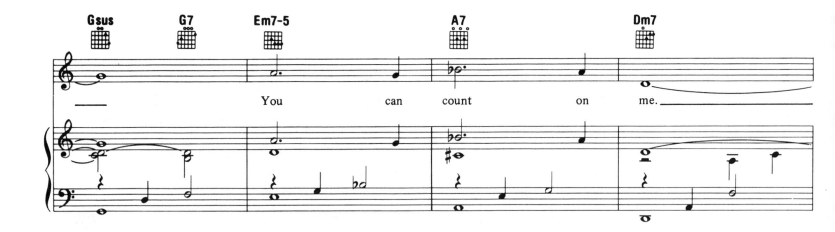

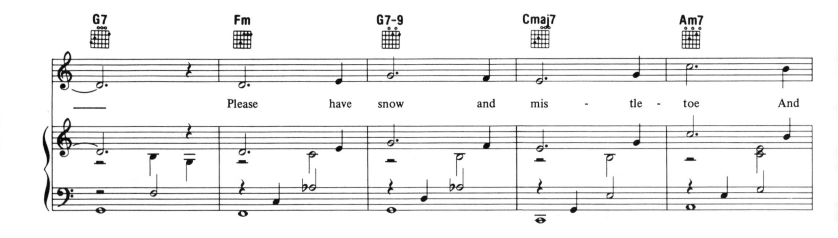

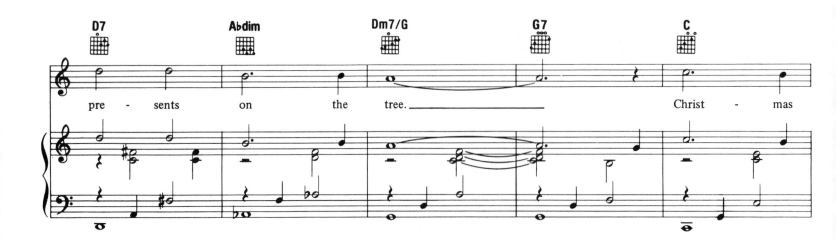

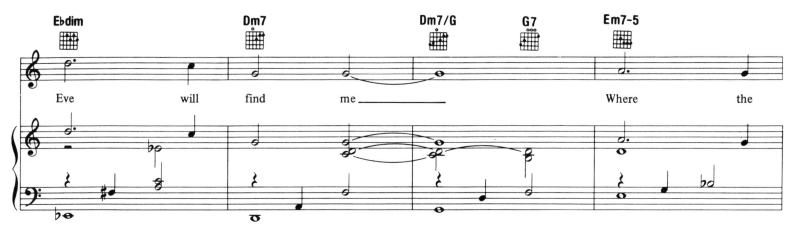

Eve will find me _____ Where the

love - light gleams, _____ I'll Be

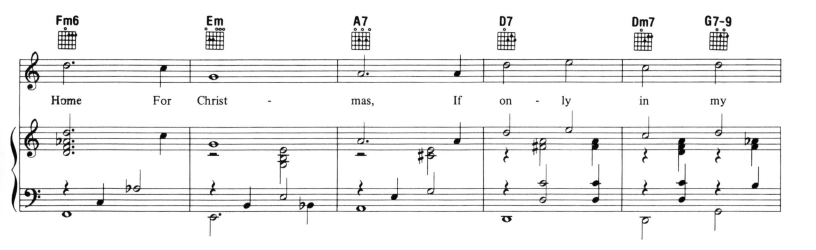

Home For Christ - mas, If on - ly in my

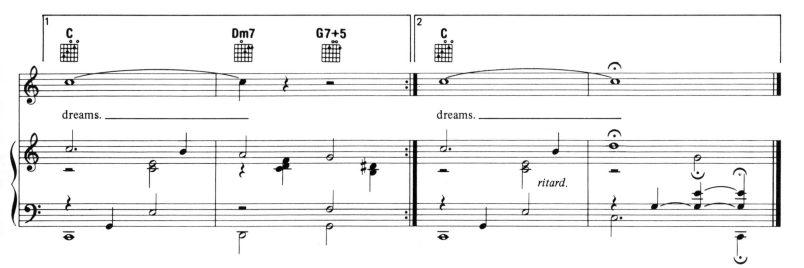

dreams. _____   dreams. _____

IT CAME UPON THE MIDNIGHT CLEAR

Words by EDMUND H. SEARS
Music by RICHARD S. WILLIS

Quietly

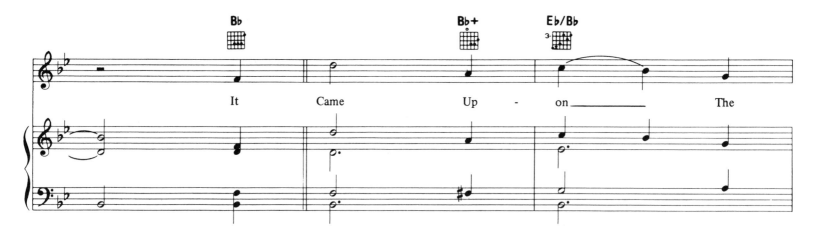

It Came Up - on _____ The

Mid - night Clear, That glo - rious

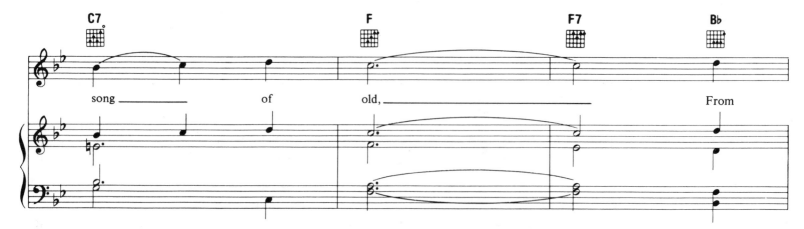

song _____ of old, _____ From

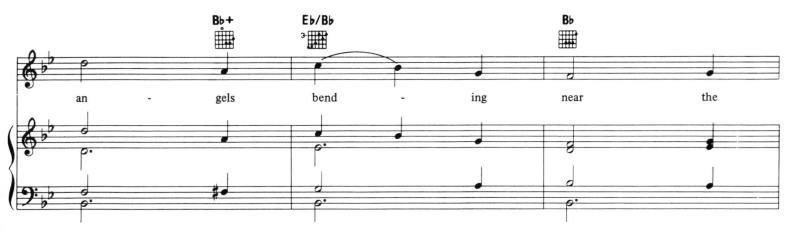

an - gels bend - ing near the

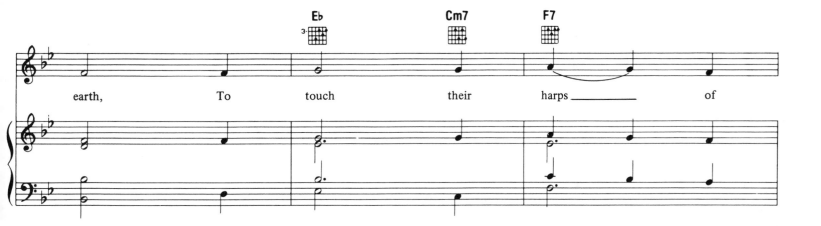

earth, To touch their harps _____ of

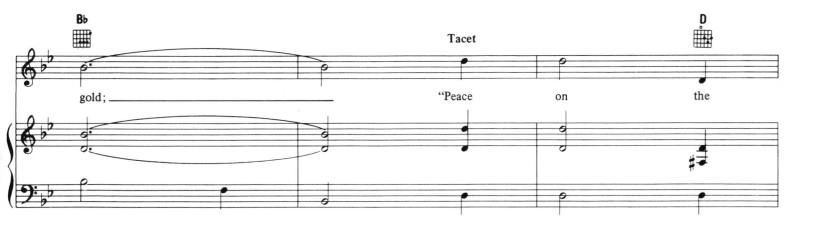

gold; _____ "Peace on the

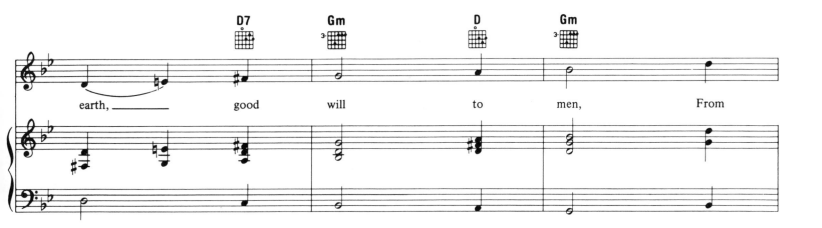

earth, _____ good will to men, From

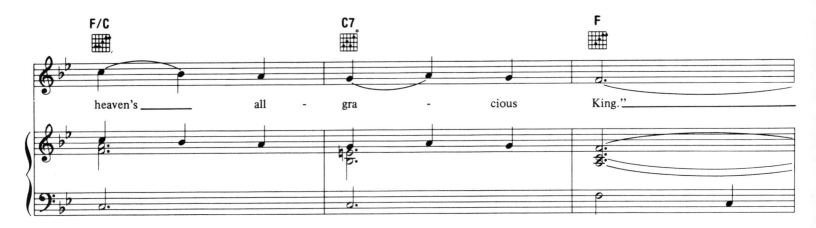

heaven's _____ all - gra - cious King." _____

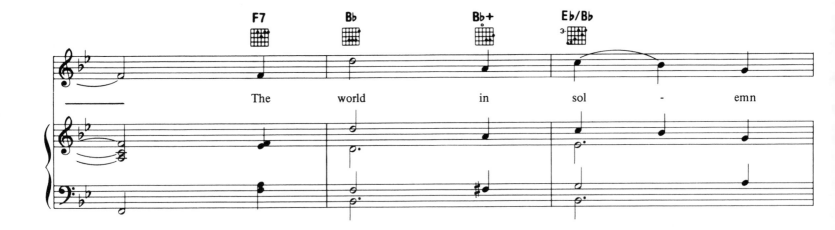

The world in sol - emn

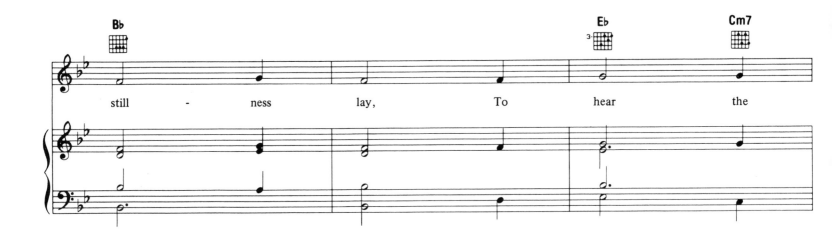

still - ness lay, To hear the

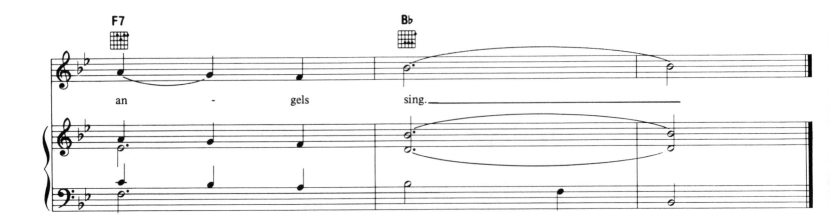

an - gels sing. _____

IT'S CHRISTMAS IN NEW YORK

Words and Music by
BILLY BUTT

JINGLE BELLS

Words and Music by
J. PIERPONT

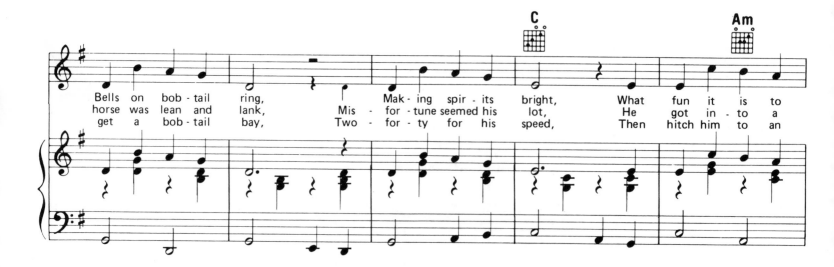

JINGLE-BELL ROCK

Words and Music by
JOE BEAL and JIM BOOTHE

Moderately (with a rock beat)

Chorus

Jin - gle-bell, Jin - gle-bell, JIN -GLE-BELL ROCK_ Jin - gle-bell swing and

Jin - gle-bells ring Snow - in' and blow-in' up bush -els of fun

JOLLY OLD ST. NICHOLAS

Traditional

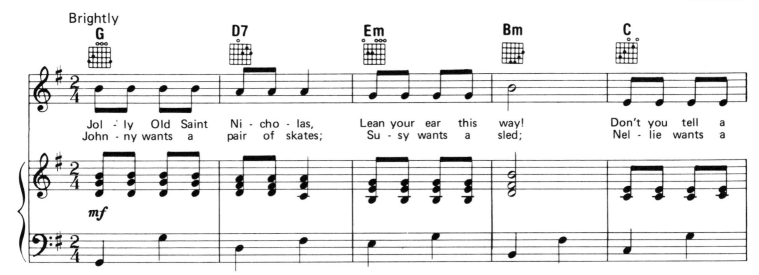

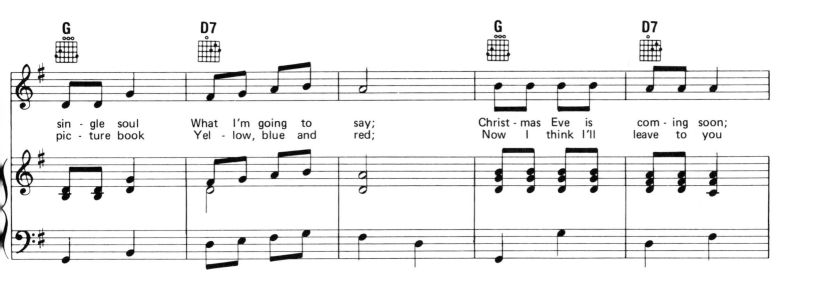

JOY TO THE WORLD

Words by ISAAC WATTS
Music by GEORGE F. HANDEL

With spirit

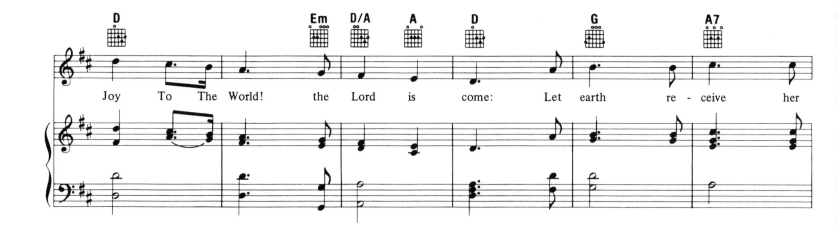

Joy To The World! the Lord is come: Let earth re - ceive her

King; Let ev - ery____ heart____ pre - pare____ Him____ room,____ And heaven and na - ture____

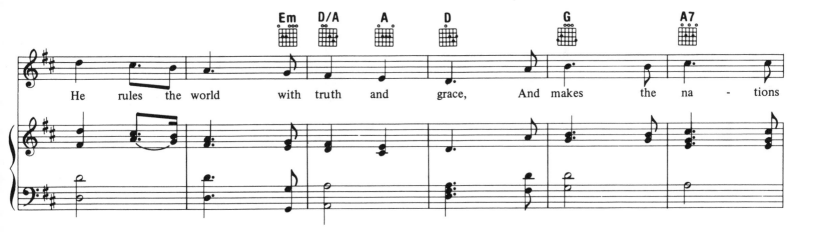

THE LAST MONTH OF THE YEAR
(What Month Was Jesus Born In?)

Words and Music by VERA HALL
Adapted and Arranged by
RUDY PICKENS TARTT and ALAN LOMAX

What month was my Je - sus born in?}
Well, they laid Him in a man - ger,} Last month of the year!

What month was my Je - sus born in?}
Well, they laid Him in the man - ger,} Last month of the year! Oh,

Jan - u - ar - y, Feb - ru - ar - y, March,

(Jan - u - ar - y) (Feb - ru - ar - y)

year!___ Oh, Jan-u-ar-y, Feb-ru-ar-y, March___

(Jan-u-ar-y) (Feb-ru-ary)

A-pril, May, June, O Lord,__you got Ju - ly, Aug-ust, Sep - tem-ber, Oc - to-ber and-a No -

vem - ber, On the twen-ty-fifth day of De - cem-ber in the last month__ of the

year.___ Well, last month__ of the year._____

MY FAVORITE THINGS

(From "THE SOUND OF MUSIC")

Lyrics by OSCAR HAMMERSTEIN II
Music by RICHARD RODGERS

LET IT SNOW! LET IT SNOW! LET IT SNOW!

Words by SAMMY CAHN
Music by JULE STYNE

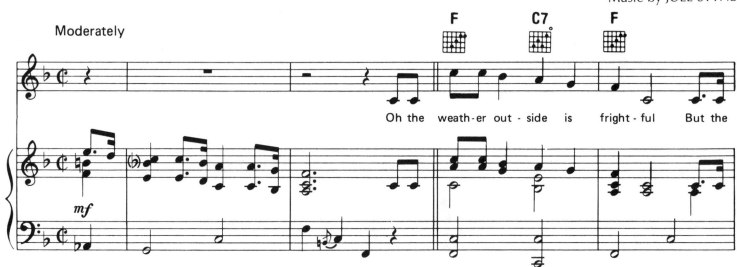

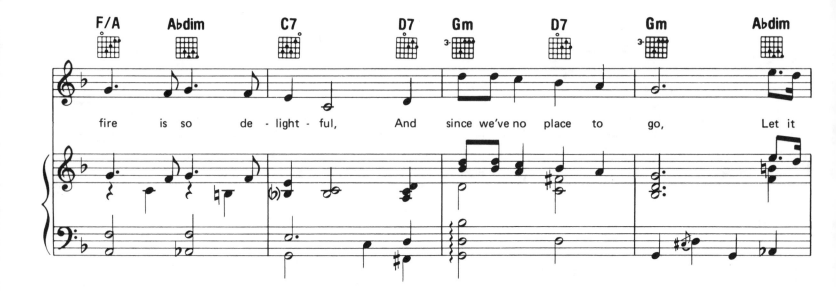

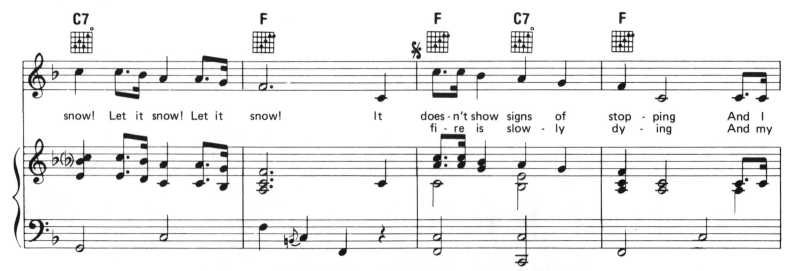

MARCH OF THE TOYS

By VICTOR HERBERT

With Spirit

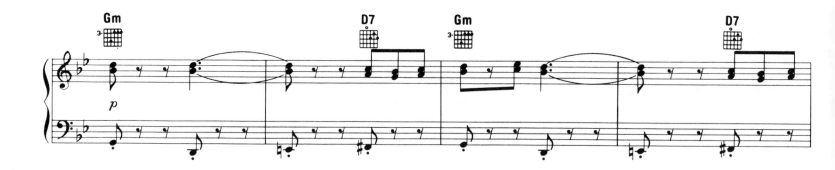

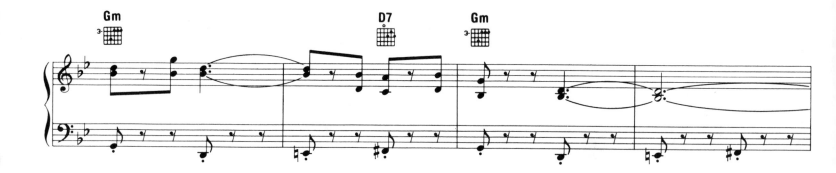

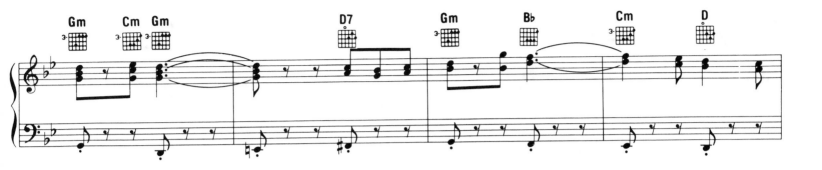

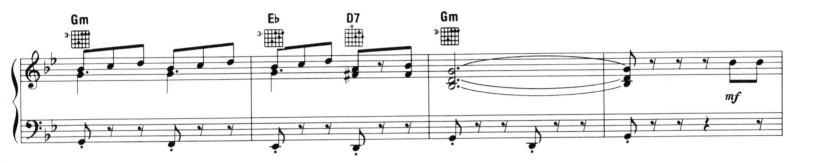

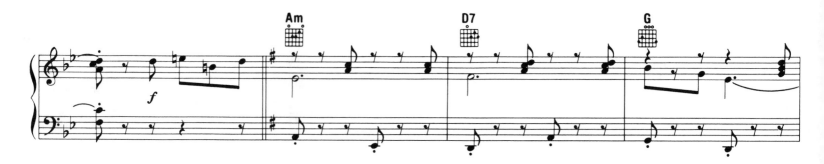

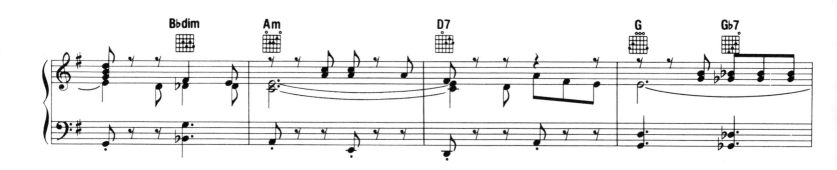

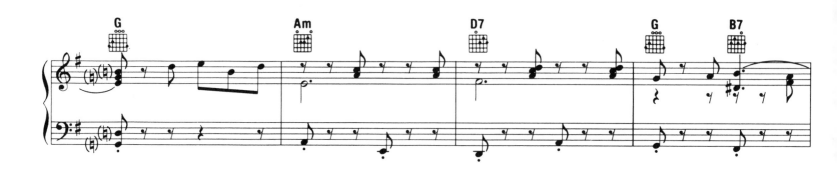

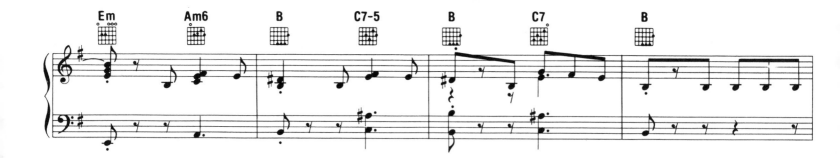

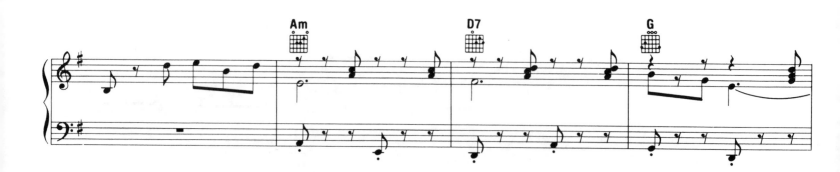

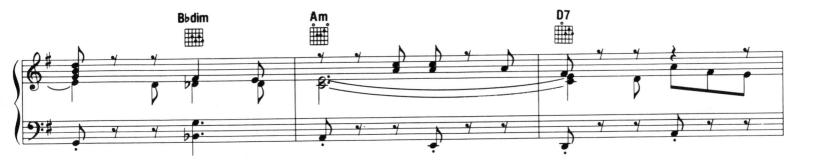

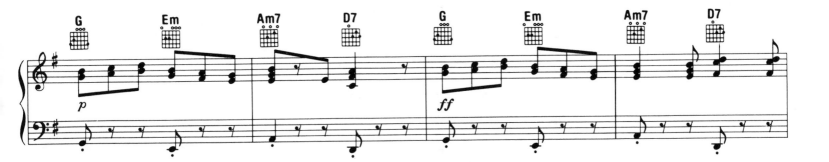

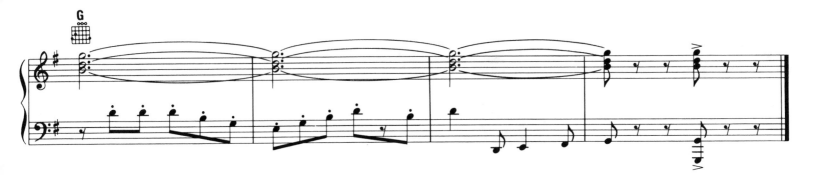

A MARSHMALLOW WORLD

Words by CARL SIGMAN
Music by PETER DE ROSE

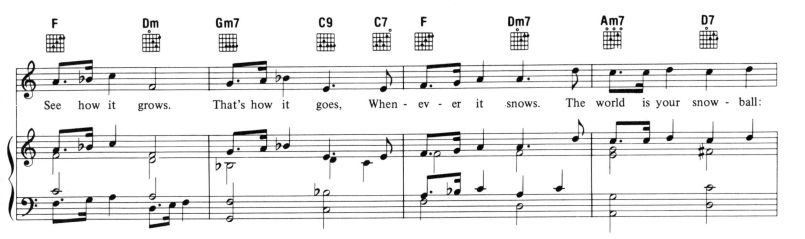

See how it grows. That's how it goes, When-ev-er it snows. The world is your snow-ball:

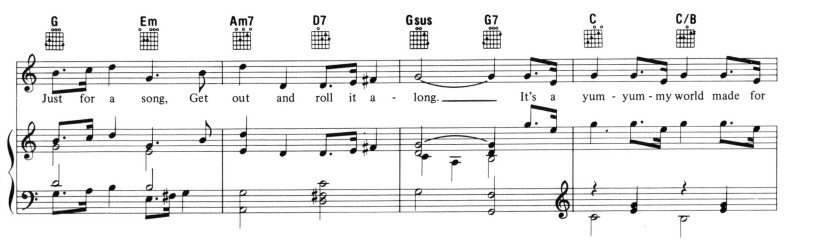

Just for a song, Get out and roll it a-long.____ It's a yum-yum-my world made for

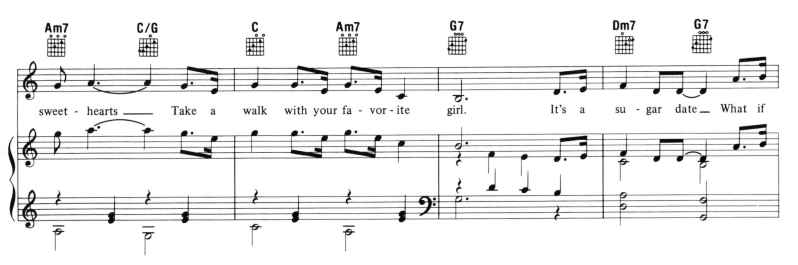

sweet-hearts ____ Take a walk with your fa-vor-ite girl. It's a su-gar date__ What if

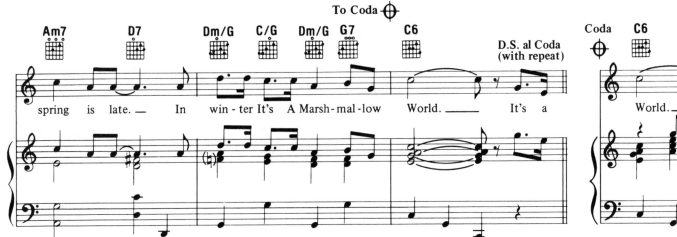

spring is late.__ In win-ter It's A Marsh-mal-low World.____ It's a

World.____

THE MOST WONDERFUL DAY OF THE YEAR

Music and Lyrics by
JOHNNY MARKS

Moderately

Ad Lib

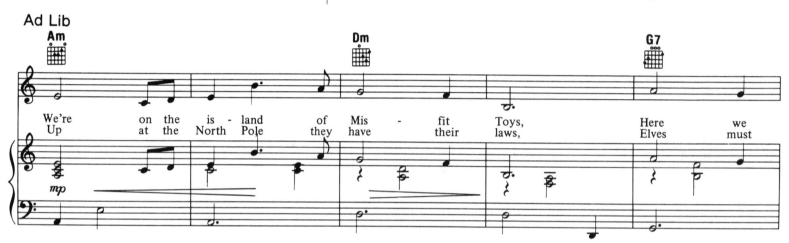

We're on the is - land of Mis - fit Toys, Here we
Up at the North Pole they have their laws, Elves we must

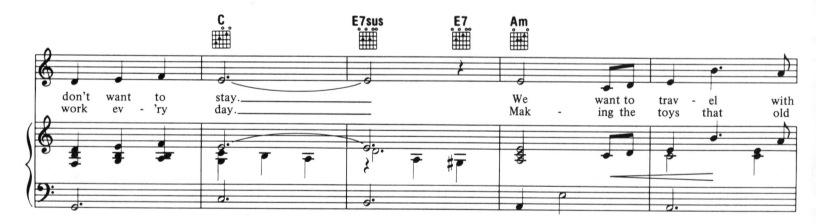

don't want to stay._____ We want to trav - el with
work ev - 'ry day._____ Mak - ing the toys that old

Moderately

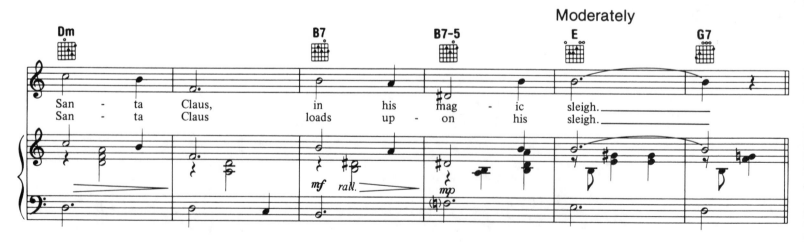

San - ta Claus, in his mag - ic sleigh._____
San - ta Claus loads up - on his sleigh._____

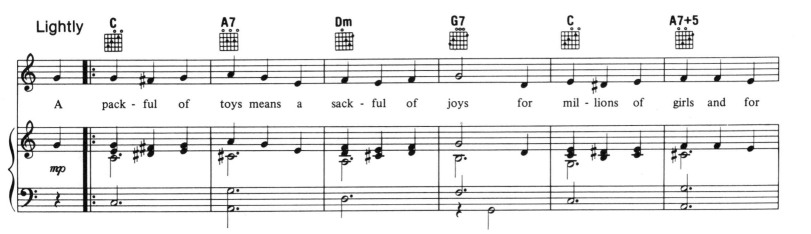

A pack-ful of toys means a sack-ful of joys for mil-lions of girls and for

mil-lions of boys when Christ-mas Day is here_____ The Most

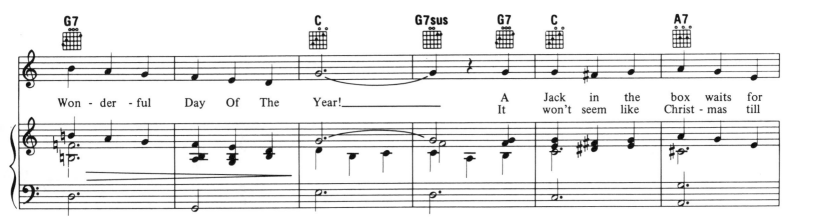

Won-der-ful Day Of The Year!_____ A It won't seem like Christ-mas till

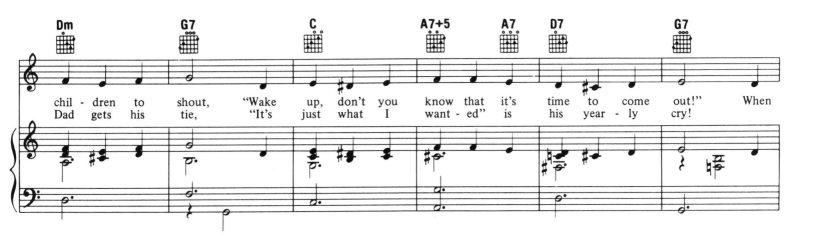

chil-dren to shout, "Wake up, don't you know that it's time to come out!" When
Dad gets his tie, "It's just what I want-ed" is his year-ly cry!

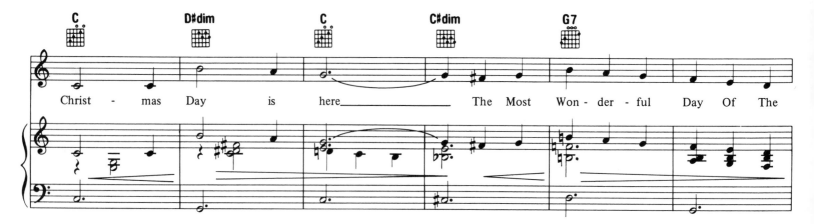

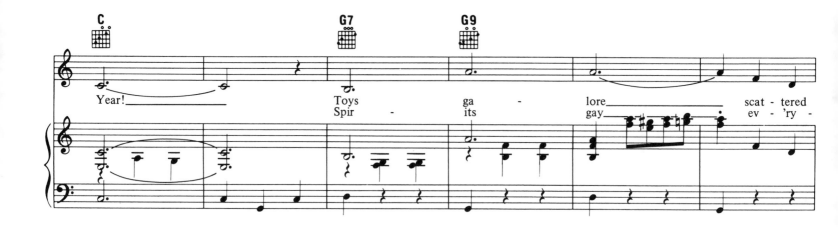

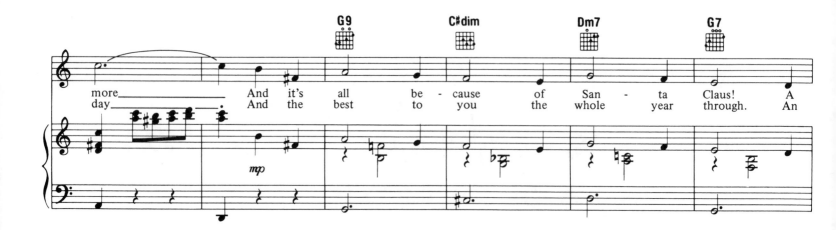

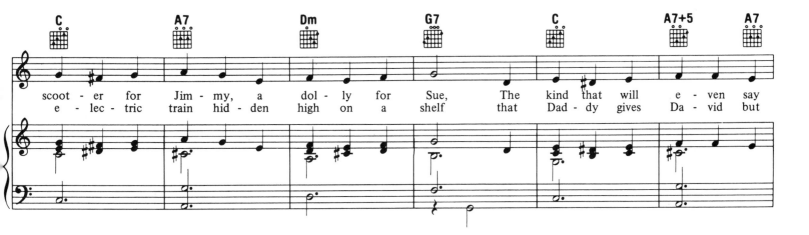

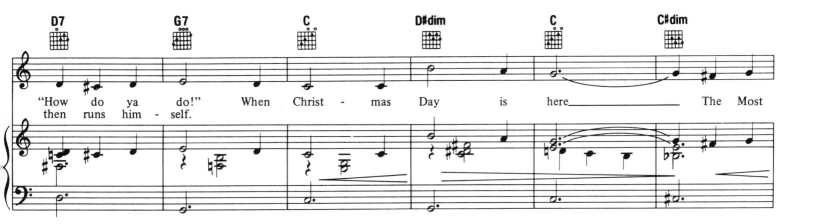

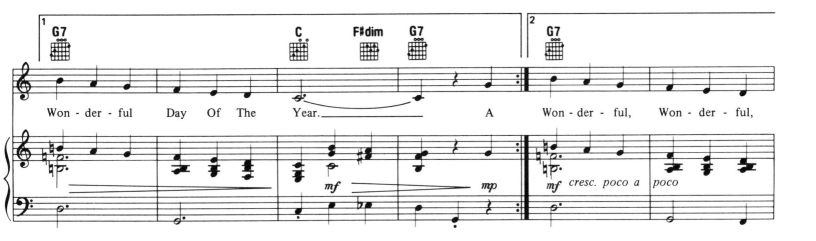

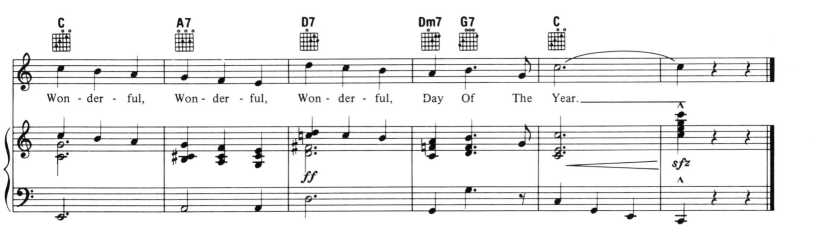

THE NIGHT BEFORE CHRISTMAS SONG

Music by JOHNNY MARKS
Lyrics adapted by JOHNNY MARKS
from CLEMENT MOORE's Poem

Gaily

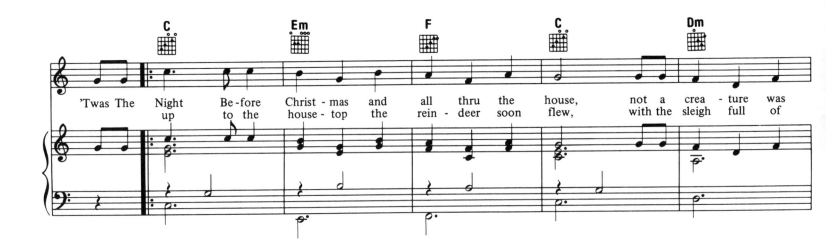

'Twas The Night Be-fore Christ-mas and all thru the house, not a crea-ture was
up to the house-top the rein-deer soon flew, with the sleigh full of

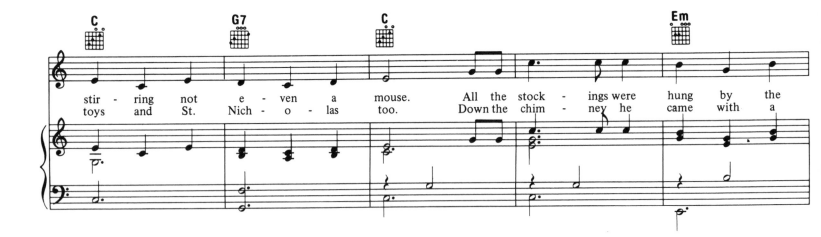

stir-ring not e-ven a mouse. All the stock-ings were hung by the
toys and St. Nich-o-las too. Down the chim-ney he came with a

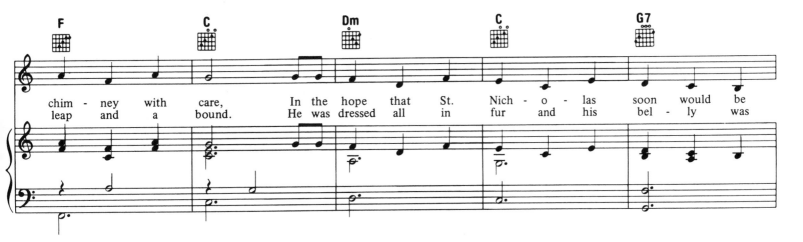

chim - ney with care,
leap and with a bound.
In the hope that St. Nich - o - las soon would be
He was dressed all in fur and his bel - ly was

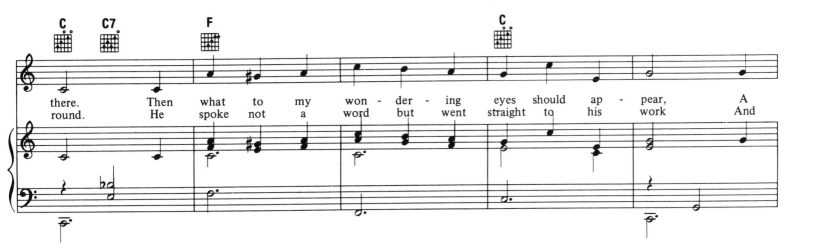

there.
round.
Then what to my won - der - ing eyes should ap - pear, A
He spoke not a word but went straight to his work And

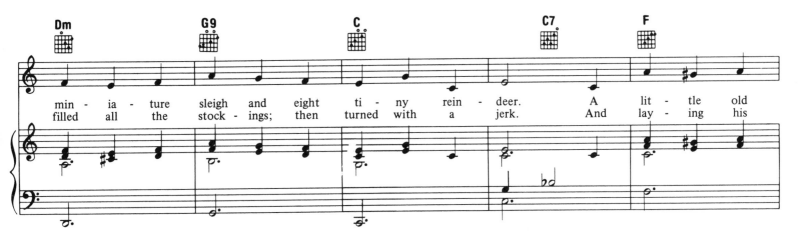

min - ia - ture sleigh and eight ti - ny rein - deer. A lit - tle old
filled all the stock - ings; then turned with a jerk. And lay - ing his

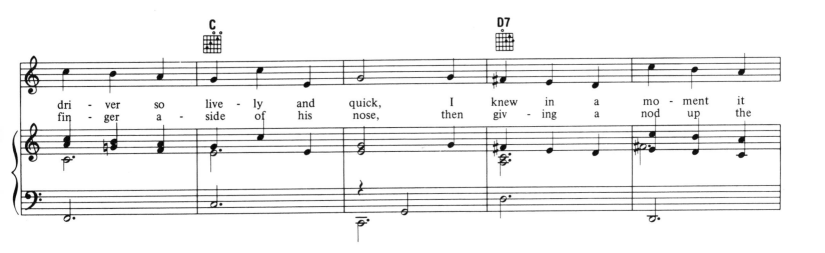

dri - ver so live - ly and quick, I knew in a mo - ment it
fin - ger a - side of his nose, then giv - ing a nod up the

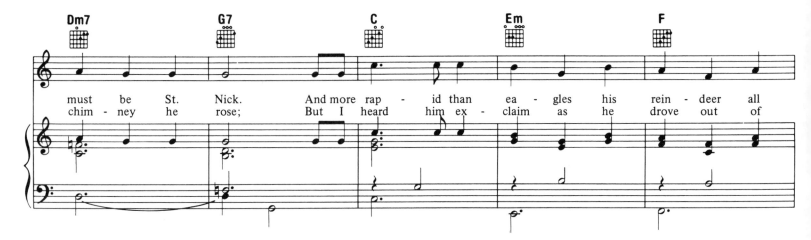

must be St. Nick. And more rap - id than ea - gles his rein - deer all
chim - ney he rose; But I heard him ex - claim as he drove out of

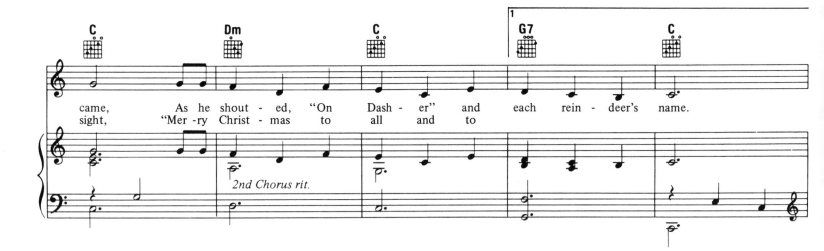

came, As he shout - ed, "On Dash - er" and each rein - deer's name.
sight, "Mer -ry Christ - mas to all and to

2nd Chorus rit.

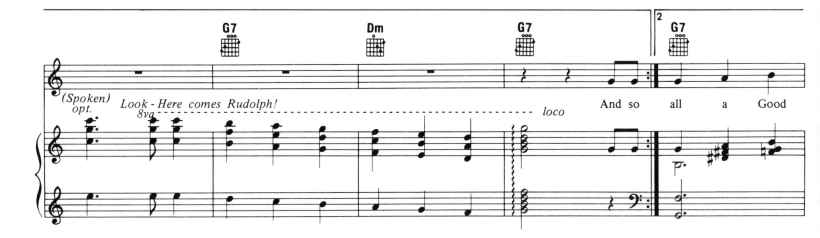

(Spoken) opt. *Look - Here comes Rudolph!* *loco*
8va

And so all a Good

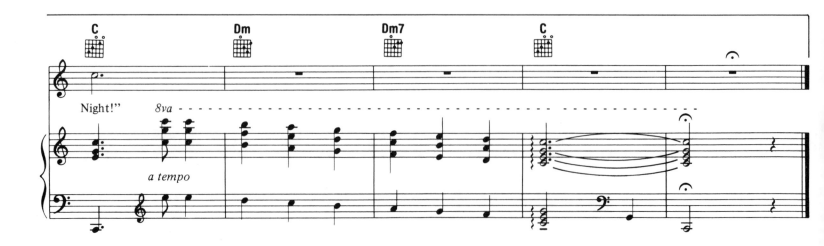

Night!" *8va*

a tempo

NUTTIN' FOR CHRISTMAS

Words and Music by
ROY BENNETT and SID TEPPER

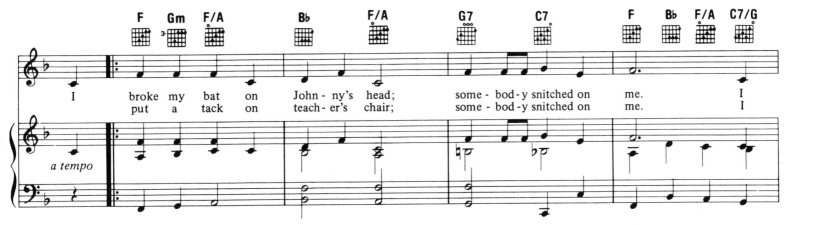

I broke my bat on John-ny's head; some-bod-y snitched on me. I
put a tack on teach-er's chair; some-bod-y snitched on me. I

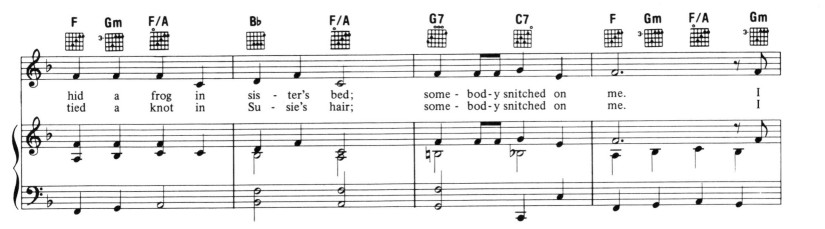

hid a frog in sis-ter's bed; some-bod-y snitched on me. I
tied a knot in Su-sie's hair; some-bod-y snitched on me. I

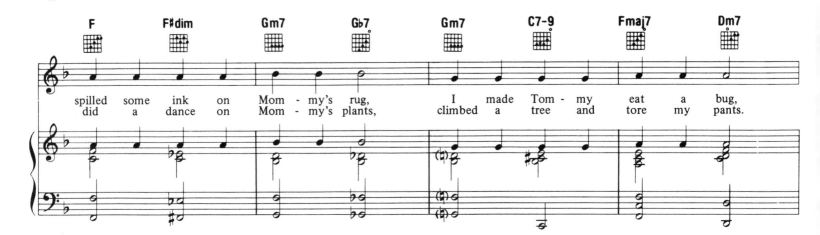

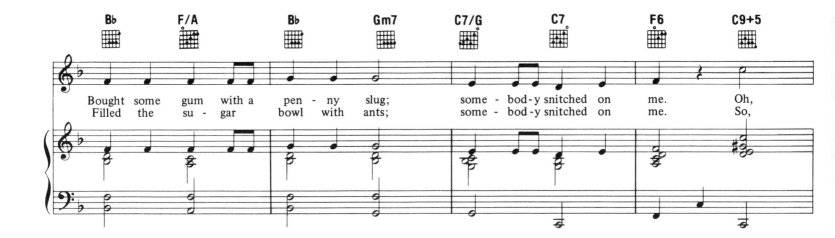

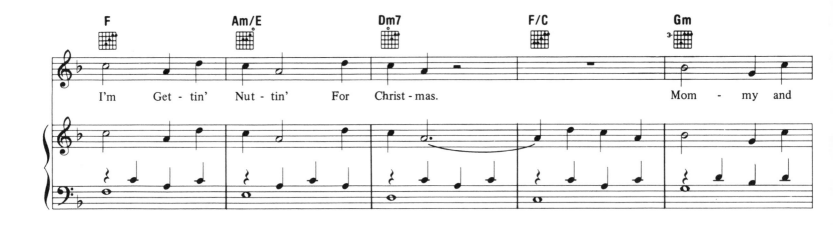

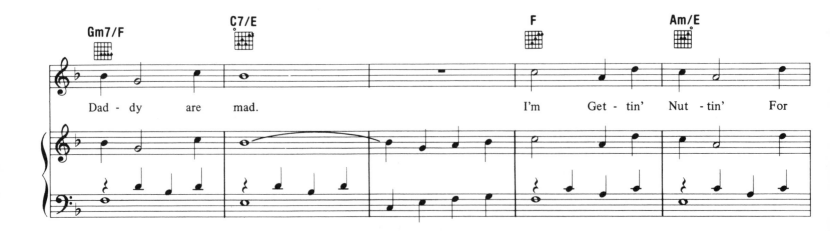

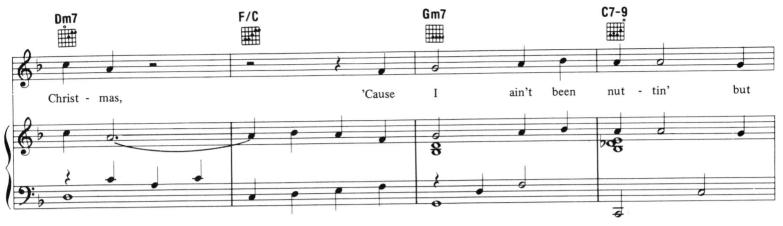

Christ - mas,   'Cause I ain't been nut - tin' but

bad. _____ I bad. _____ So you

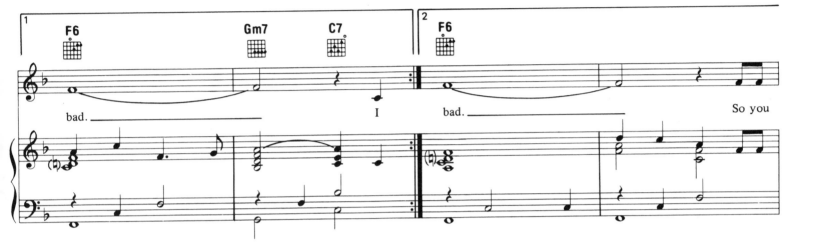

bet - ter be good, what ev - er you do, 'cause if you're bad I'm warn - ing you,

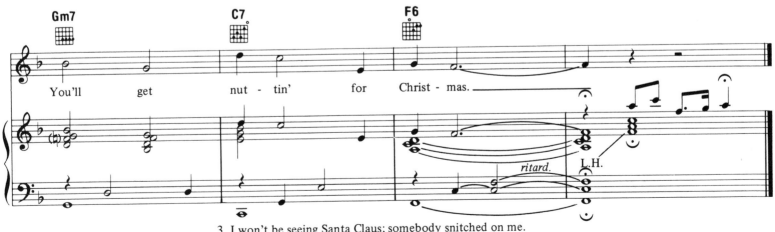

You'll get nut - tin' for Christ - mas. _____

3. I won't be seeing Santa Claus; somebody snitched on me.
He won't come visit me because somebody snitched on me.
Next year I'll be going straight, next year I'll be good, just wait,
I'd start now but it's too late; somebody snitched on me. Oh,

O CHRISTMAS TREE

German

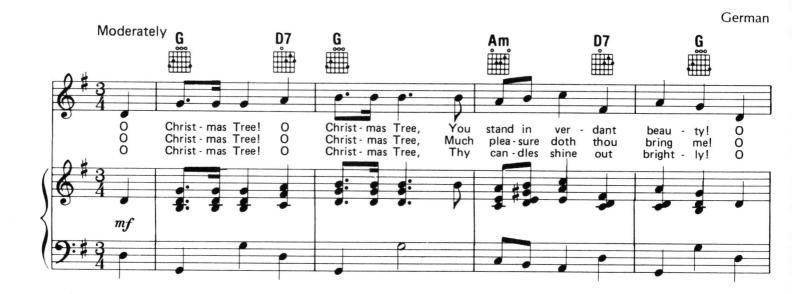

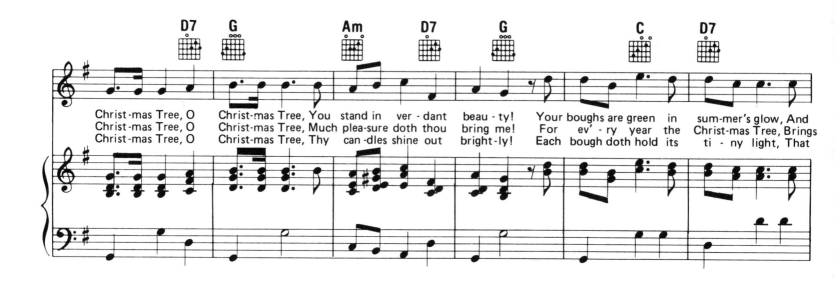

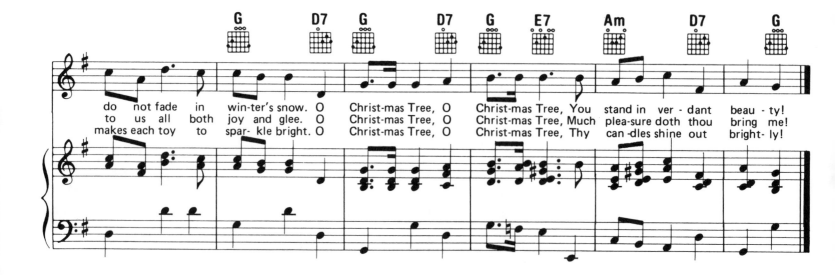

O LITTLE TOWN OF BETHLEHEM

Words by PHILLIPS BROOKS
Music by LEWIS H. REDNER

Quietly

O   Lit - tle Town Of
For   Christ is born of

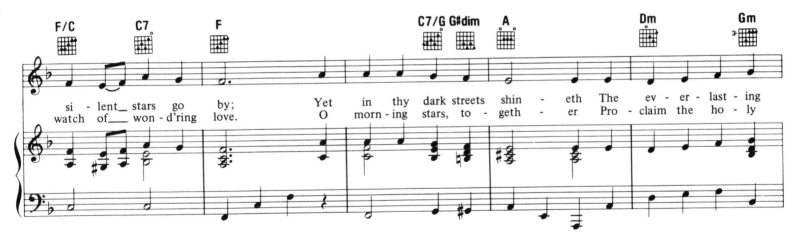

Beth - le - hem, How   still we __ see thee   lie!   A - bove thy deep and   dream - less sleep The
Ma - ry, And   gath - ered __ all a - bove,   While   mor - tals sleep the   an - gels   keep Their

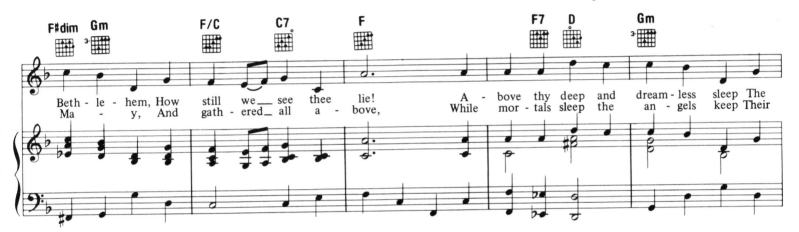

si - lent __ stars go   by;   Yet   in thy dark streets shin - eth The ev - er - last - ing
watch of __ won - d'ring love.   O   morn - ing stars, to - geth - er Pro - claim the ho - ly

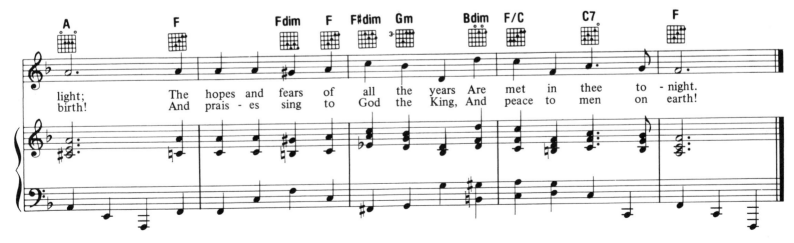

light;   The hopes and fears of   all the years Are   met in   thee   to - night.
birth!   And prais - es sing to   God the King, And   peace to men   on   earth!

O COME ALL YE FAITHFUL
(ADESTE FIDELIS)

Latin Words translated by
FREDERICK OAKELEY
Music by JOHN READING

Triumphantly

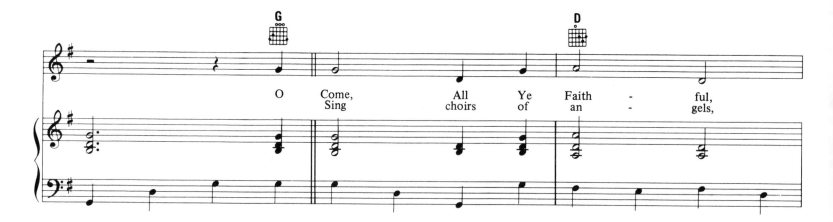

O Come, All Ye Faith - ful,
Sing choirs of an - gels,

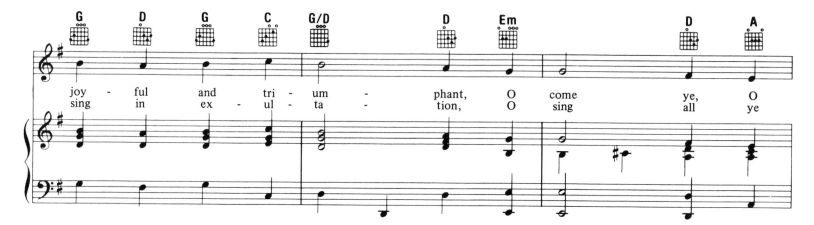

joy - ful and tri - um - phant, O come ye, O
sing in ex - ul - ta - tion, O come sing all ye

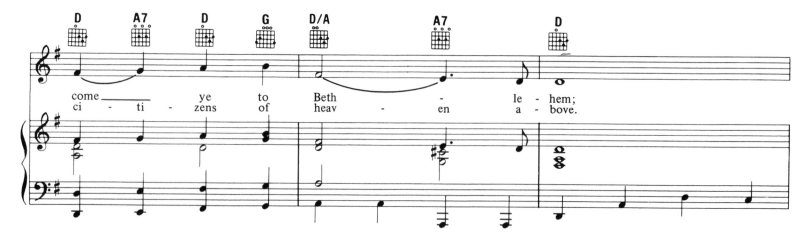

come ___ ye to Beth - le - hem;
ci - ti - zens of heav - en a - bove.

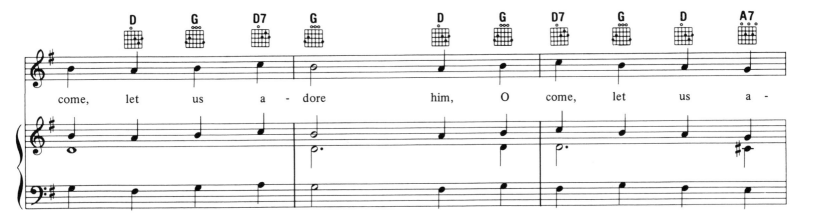

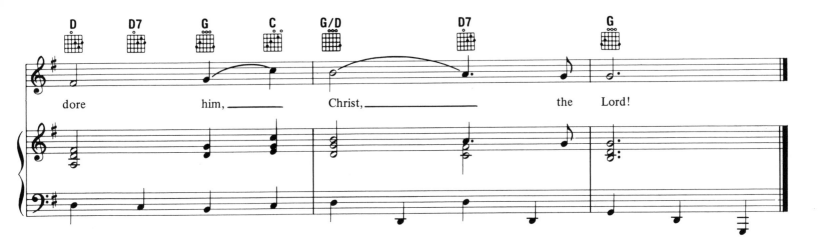

O HOLY NIGHT

English Words by D.S. DWIGHT
Music by ADOLPHE ADAM

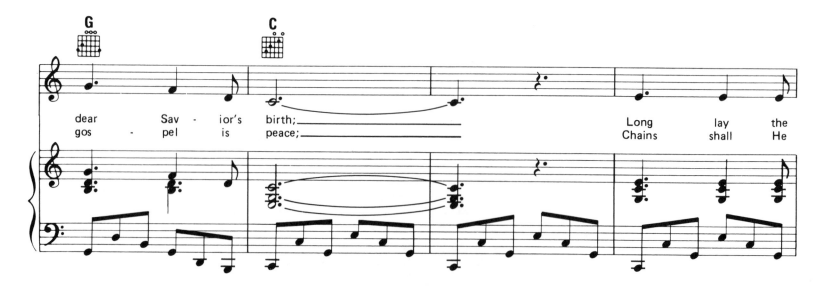

OLD TOY TRAINS

Words and Music by
ROGER MILLER

PARADE OF THE WOODEN SOLDIERS

English Lyrics by BALLARD MacDONALD
Music by LEON JESSEL

Wood - en sol - diers on pa - rade. Day-light is creep - ing, Dol-lies are sleep - ing,

In the toy - shop win - dow fast; Sol - diers so jol - ly, Think of each dol - ly, Dream - ing of the

night that's past; When in the morn - ing, with - out a warn - ing, Toy - man pulls the

win - dow shade, There's no sign the Wood bri - gade was ev - er out up-on pa - rade.

ONCE IN ROYAL DAVID'S CITY

Words by C.F. ALEXANDER
Music by H.J. GAUNTLETT

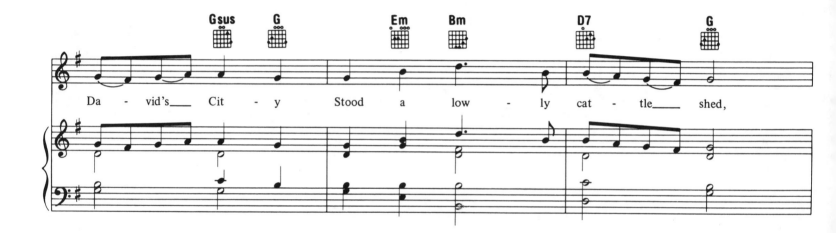

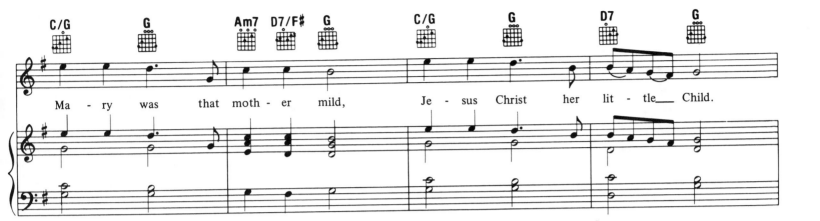

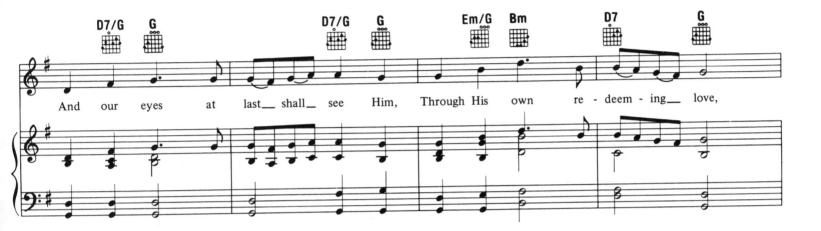

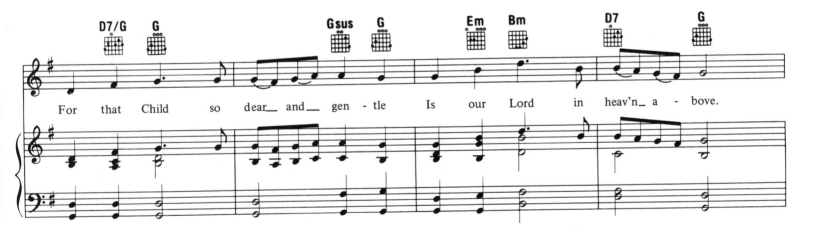

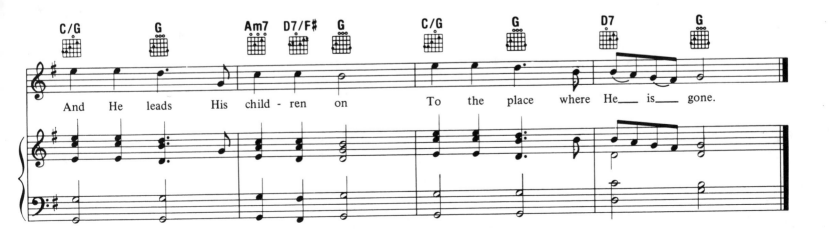

PRETTY PAPER

Words and Music by
WILLIE NELSON

Slowly, with expression

Crowd-ed streets, bus-y feet hus-tle by him. Down-town shop-pers, Christ-mas is night. There he sits all a-lone on the side-walk. Hop-ing that you won't pass him

blue. Wrap your pres - ents to your dar - ling from

you. Pret - ty pen - cils to write, "I love you."

Pret - ty pa - per, pret - ty rib - bons of blue. Pret - ty

blue.

ROCKIN' AROUND THE CHRISTMAS TREE

Music and Lyrics by
JOHNNY MARKS

Moderately with a Rock

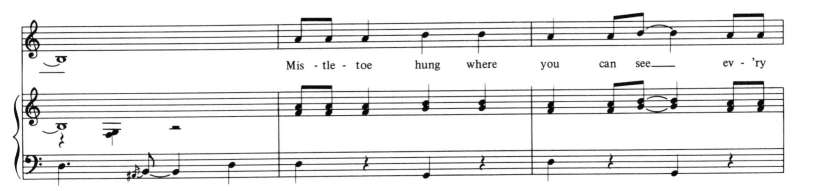

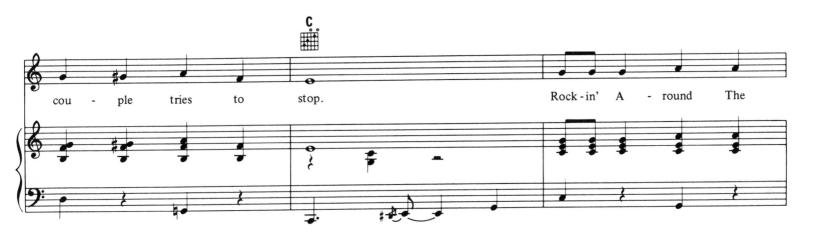

Christ - mas Tree,___ let the Christ - mas spir - it ring.___

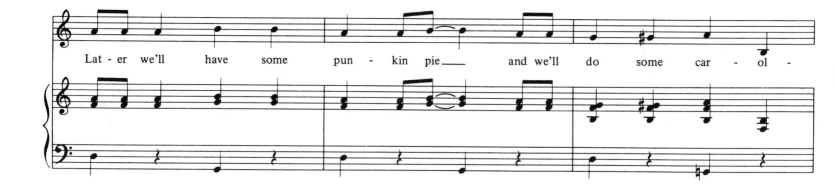

Lat - er we'll have some pun - kin pie___ and we'll do some car - ol -

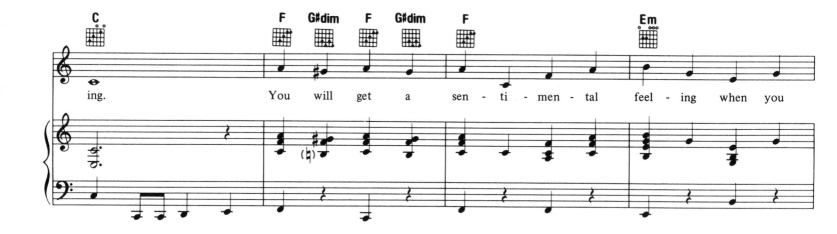

ing. You will get a sen - ti - men - tal feel - ing when you

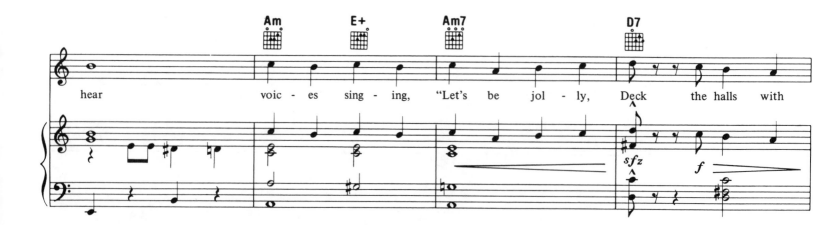

hear voic - es sing - ing, "Let's be jol - ly, Deck the halls with

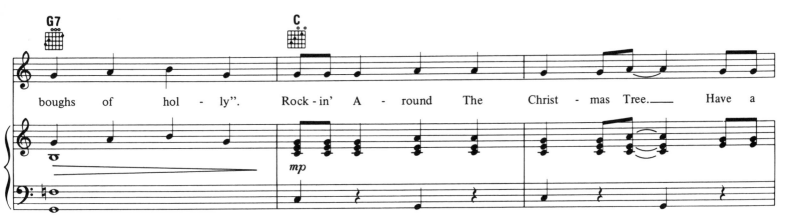

boughs of hol - ly". Rock-in' A - round The Christ - mas Tree.___ Have a

hap - py hol - i - day.___ Ev-'ry-one danc - ing mer - ri - ly___ in the

new old fash - ioned way.   new old fash - ioned

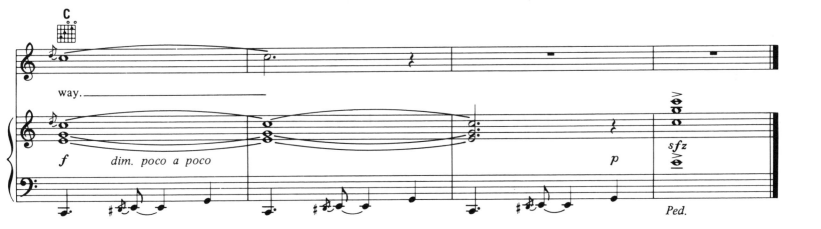

way.___

RUDOLPH THE RED-NOSED REINDEER

Music and Lyrics by
JOHNNY MARKS

You know Dash-er and Danc-er and Pranc-er and Vix-en, Com-et and Cu-pid and Don-ner and Blitz-en,

but do you re - call the most fa - mous rein-deer of all.

Ru-dolph, The Red - Nosed Rein - deer had a ver - y shin - y nose,

and if you ev - er saw it, you would e - ven say it glows.

All of the oth - er rein - deer used to laugh and call him names,

they nev - er let poor Ru - dolph join in an - y rein - deer games.

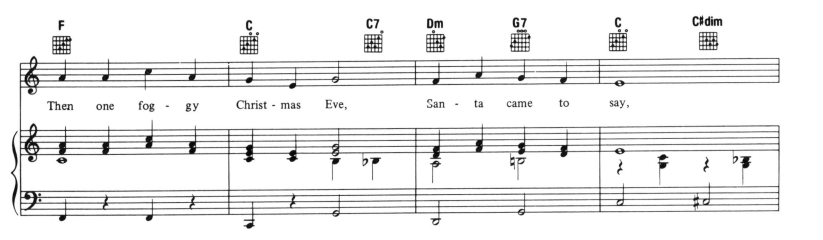

Then one fog - gy Christ - mas Eve, San - ta came to say,

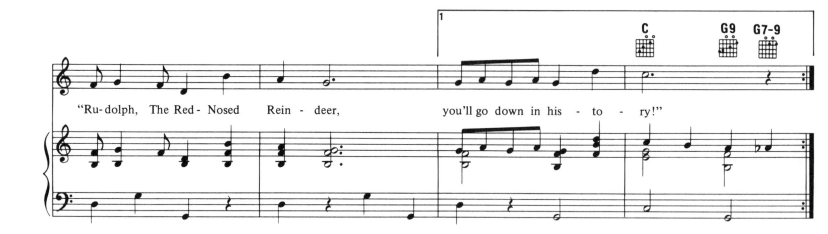

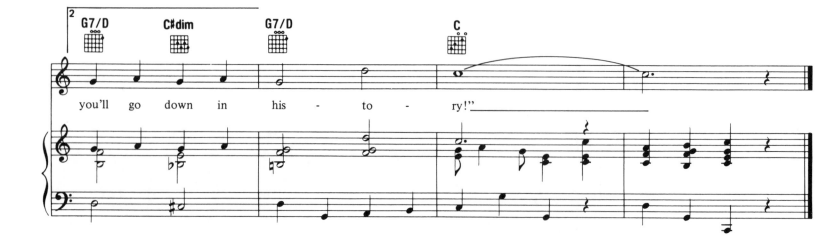

SANTA BABY

By JOAN JAVITS, PHIL SPRINGER
and TONY SPRINGER

SANTA, BRING MY BABY BACK
(TO ME)

Words and Music by
CLAUDE DeMETRUIS and AARON SCHROEDER

Bright rock

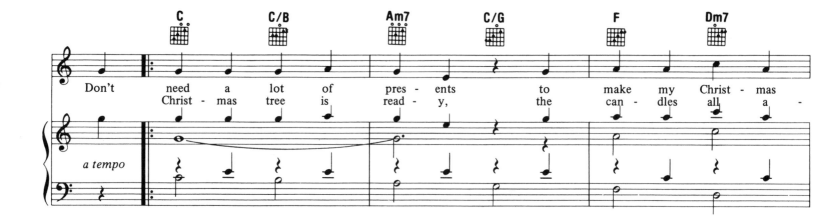

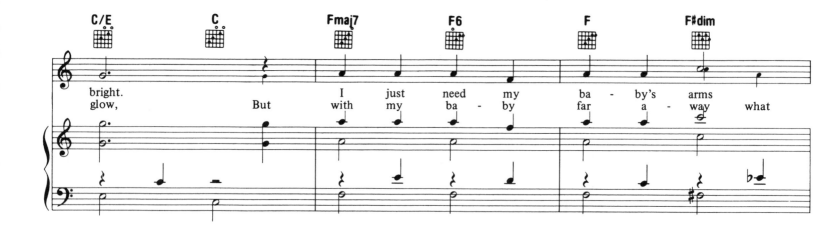

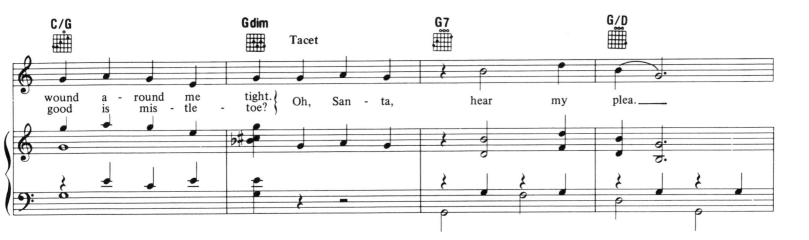

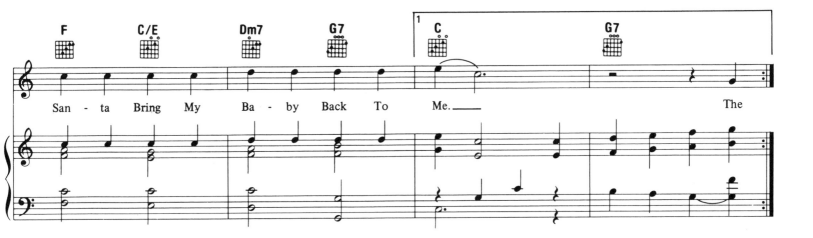

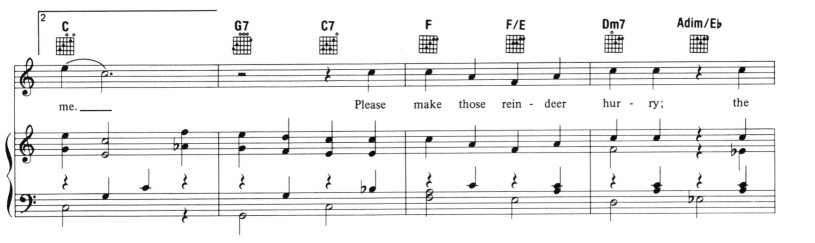

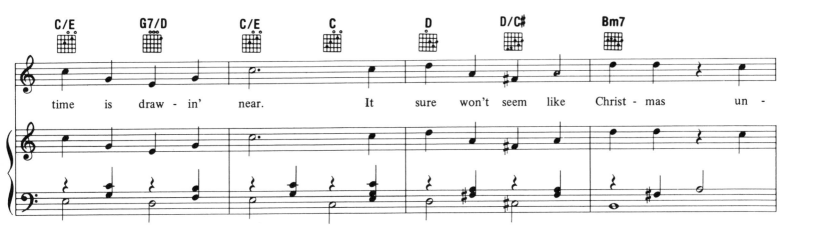

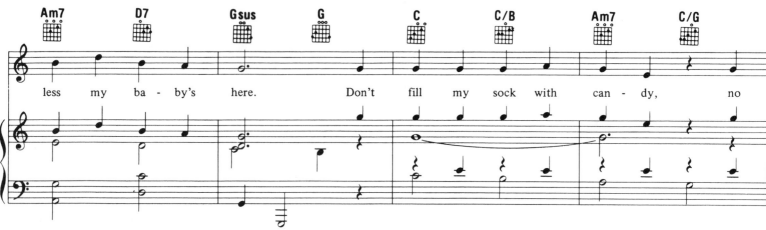

less my ba-by's here. Don't fill my sock with can-dy, no

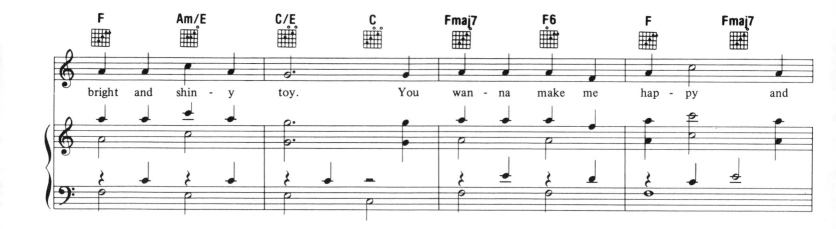

bright and shin-y toy. You wan-na make me hap-py and

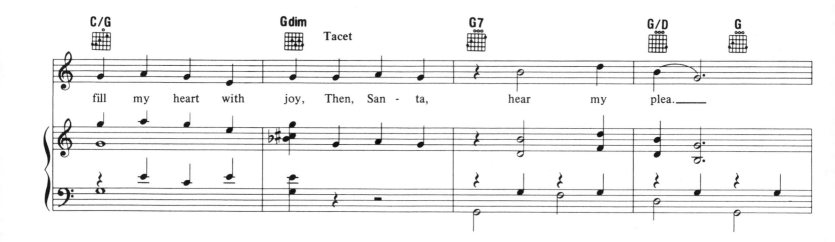

fill my heart with joy, Then, San-ta, hear my plea.____

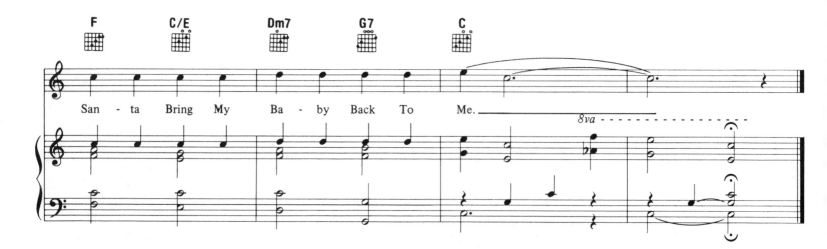

San-ta Bring My Ba-by Back To Me.____

SILVER BELLS

Words and Music by
JAY LIVINGSTON and RAY EVANS

SILENT NIGHT

Words by JOSEPH MOHR
Music by FRANZ GRÜBER

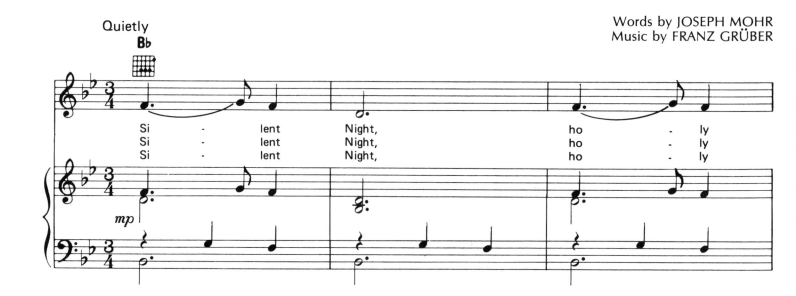

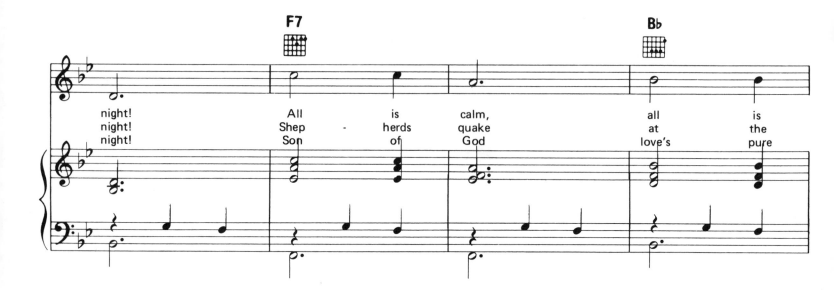

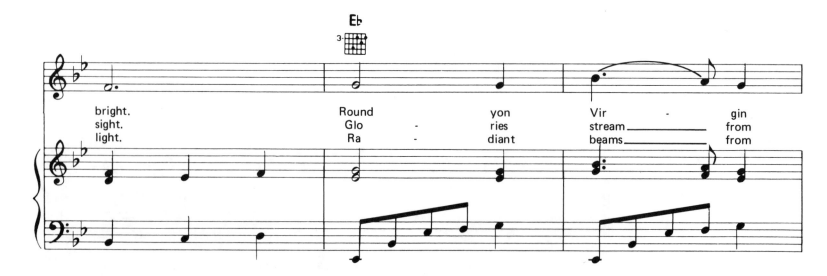

SILVER AND GOLD

Music and Lyrics by
JOHNNY MARKS

Slowly and expressively

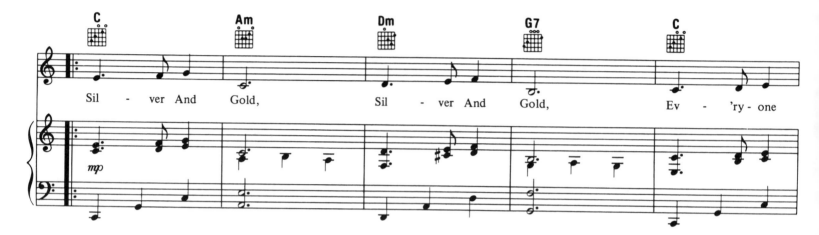

Sil - ver And Gold, Sil - ver And Gold, Ev - 'ry-one

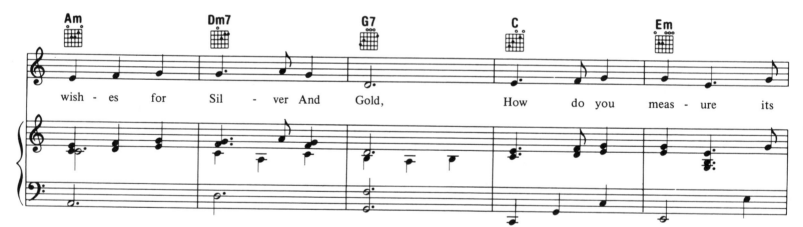

wish - es for Sil - ver And Gold, How do you meas - ure its

worth?_____ Just by the pleas - ure it gives here on

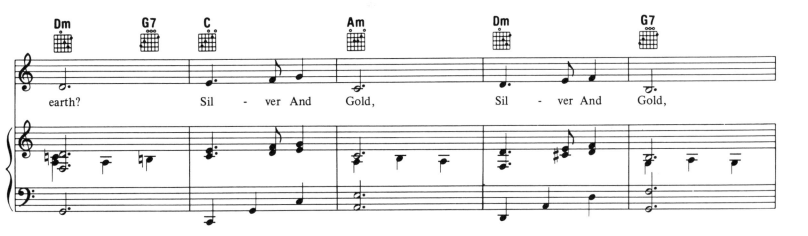

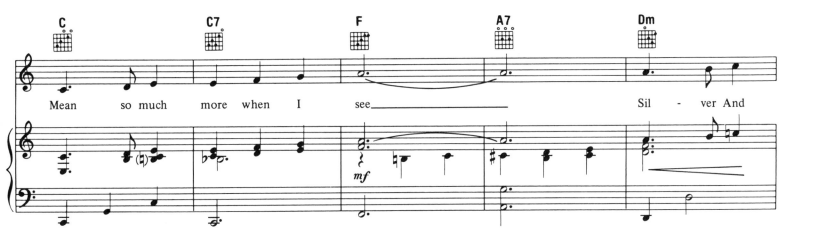

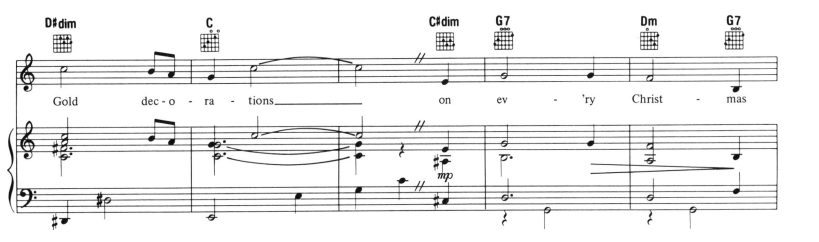

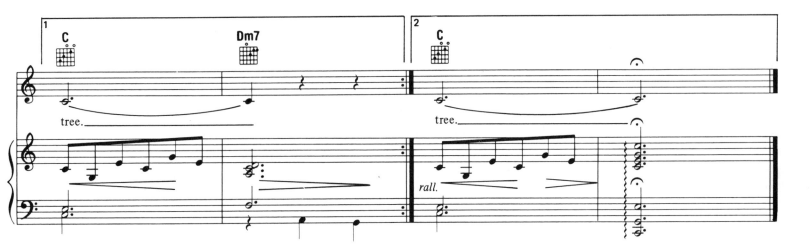

THE STAR CAROL

Lyric by WIHLA HUTSON
Music by ALFRED BURT

Tenderly with much expression

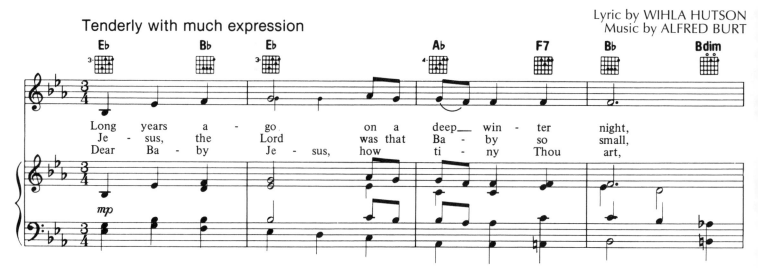

Long years a-go on a deep win-ter night,
Je-sus, the Lord was that Ba-by so small,
Dear Ba-by Je-sus, how ti-ny Thou art,

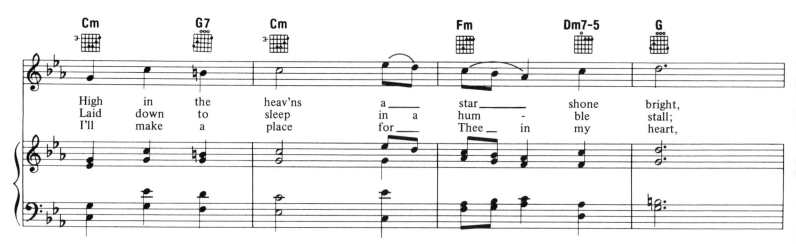

High in the heav'ns a star shone bright,
Laid down to sleep in a hum-ble stall;
I'll make a place for Thee in my heart,

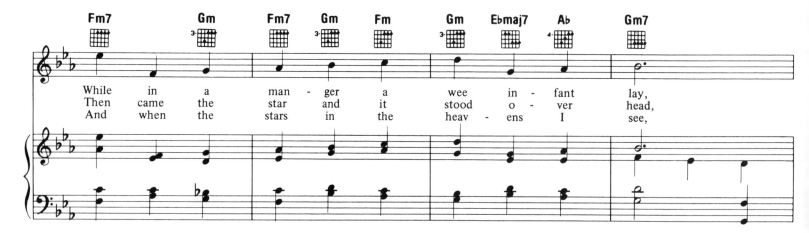

While in a man-ger a wee in-fant lay,
Then came the star and it stood o-ver head,
And when the stars in the heav-ens I see,

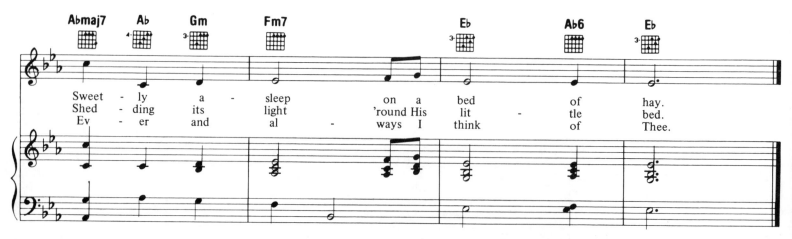

Sweet-ly a-sleep on a bed of hay.
Shed-ding its light 'round His lit-tle bed.
Ev-er and al-ways I think of Thee.

TOYLAND
(From "BABES IN TOYLAND")

Words by GLEN MAC DONOUGH
Music by VICTOR HERBERT

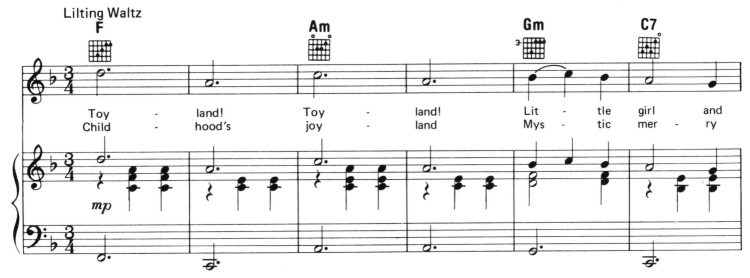

Toy - land! Toy - land! Lit - tle girl and
Child - hood's joy - land Mys - tic mer - ry

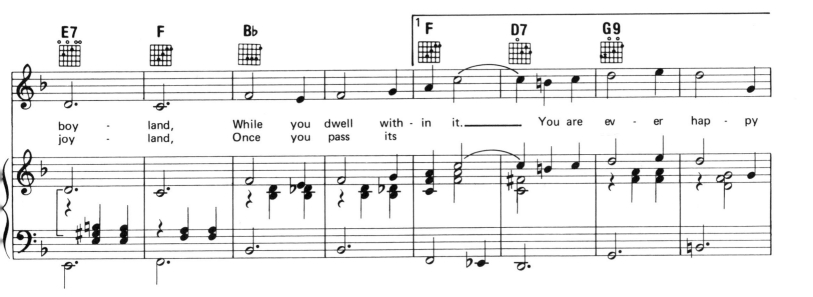

boy - land, While you dwell with - in it. ___ You are ev - er hap - py
joy - land, Once you pass its

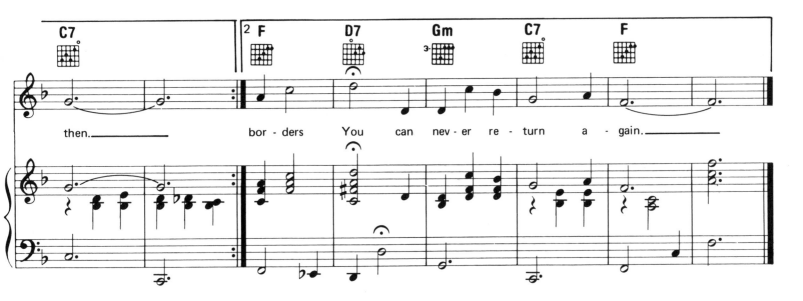

then. ___ bor - ders You can nev - er re - turn a - gain. ___

SUZY SNOWFLAKE

Words and Music by
SID TEPPER and ROY BENNETT

THAT CHRISTMAS FEELING

Words and Music by
BENNIE BENJAMIN and GEORGE WEISS

Moderately slow

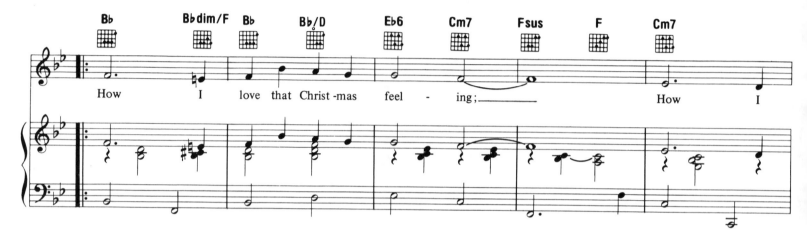

How I love that Christ-mas feel - ing; _____ How I

treas-ure its friend-ly glow. _____ See the way a stran-ger

greets you _____ Just as though you'd met him Christ-mas-es a - go. _____

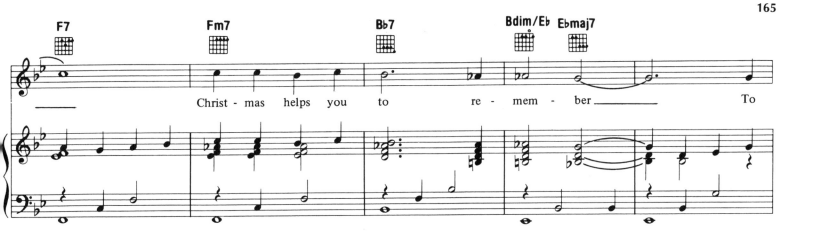

Christ - mas helps you to re - mem - ber ____ To

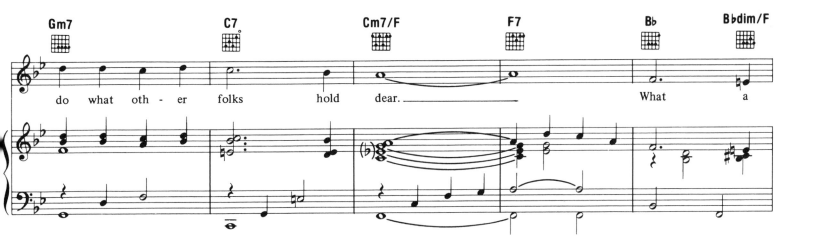

do what oth - er folks hold dear. ____ What a

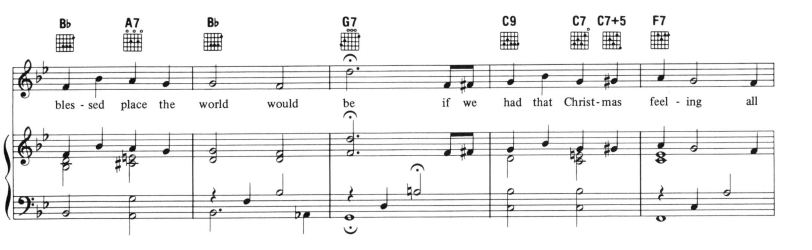

bles - sed place the world would be if we had that Christ - mas feel - ing all

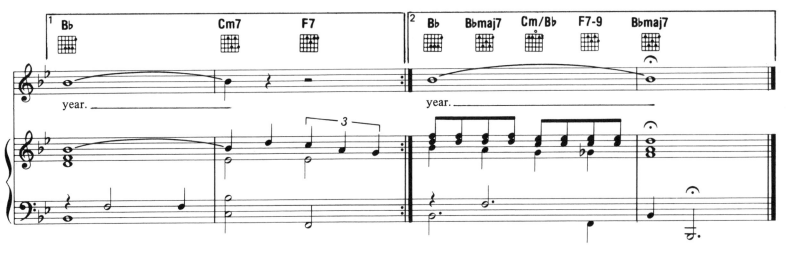

year. ____ year. ____

THERE IS NO CHRISTMAS LIKE
A HOME CHRISTMAS

Words by CARL SIGMAN
Music by MICKEY J. ADDY

Slowly

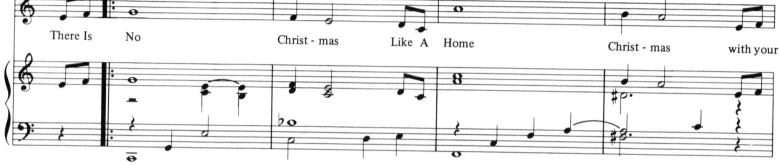

There Is No Christ - mas Like A Home Christ - mas with your

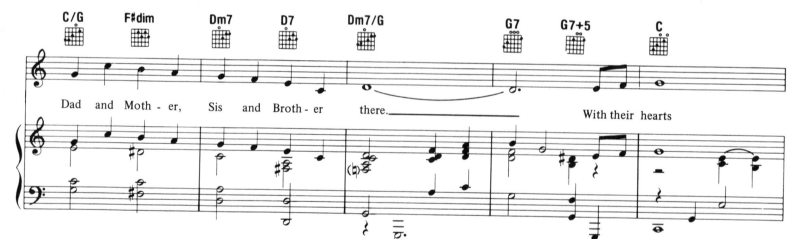

Dad and Moth - er, Sis and Broth - er there._____ With their hearts

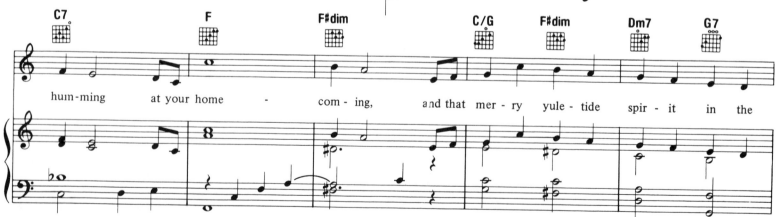

hum - ming at your home - com - ing, and that mer - ry yule - tide spir - it in the

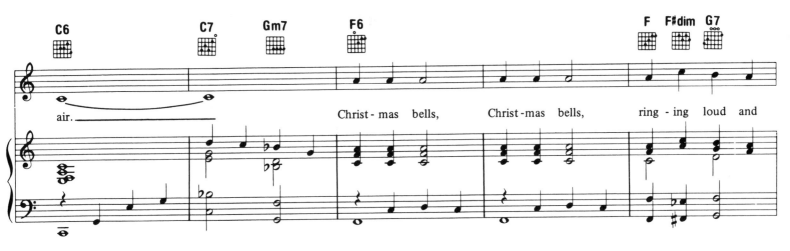

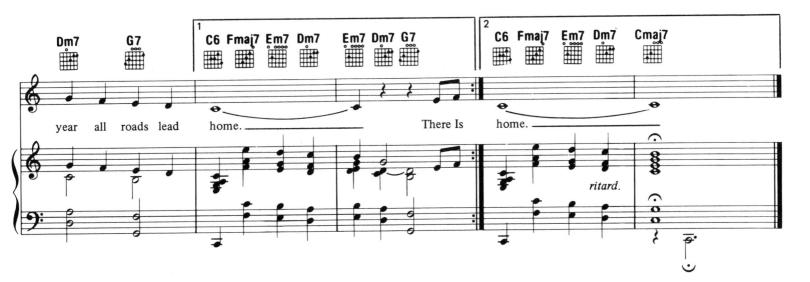

THE TWELVE DAYS OF CHRISTMAS

Traditional

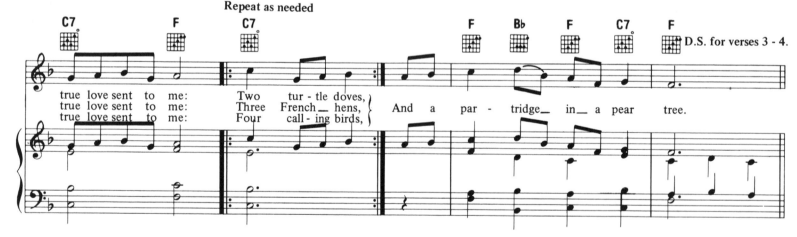

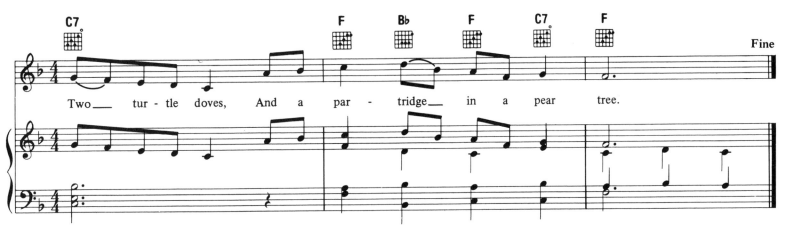

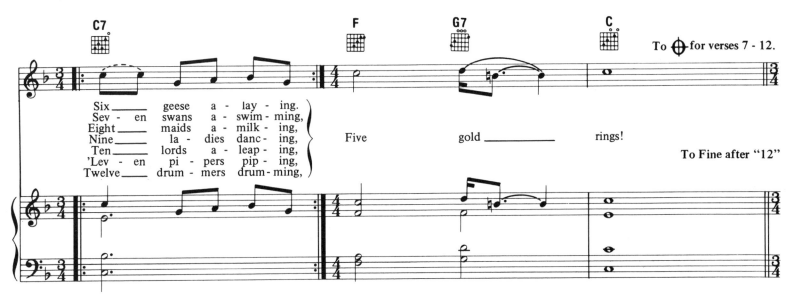

UP ON THE HOUSETOP

Traditional

Brightly

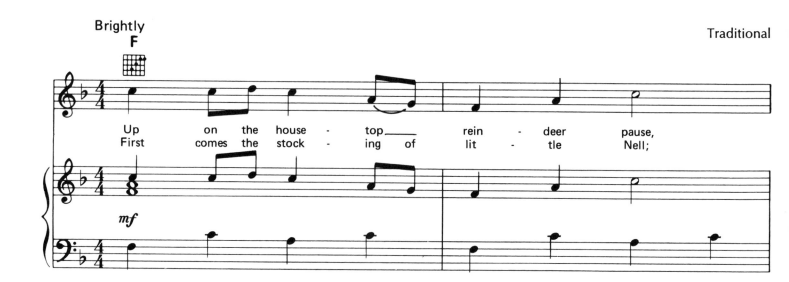

Up on the house - top____ rein - deer pause,
First comes the stock - ing of lit - tle Nell;

Out jumps good old San - ta Claus; Down thru the chim - ney with
Oh, dear good San - ta, fill it well; Give her a dol - lie that

lots of toys, All for the lit - tle ones, Christ - mas joys.
laughs and cries, One that will o - pen and shut her eyes.

WE THREE KINGS OF ORIENT ARE

Words and Music by
JOHN H. HOPKINS

Moderately

We Three Kings of O - ri - ent are;

Bear - ing gifts we tra - verse a - far,

Field and foun - tain, moor and moun - tain,

WHAT CHILD IS THIS?

English

Slow and Serene

What Child is this,_____ who, laid to rest,_____ On
So bring Him in - cense, gold and myrrh,_____ Come

Ma - ry's lap_____ is sleep - ing? Whom an - gels
peas - ant king_____ to own Him; The King of

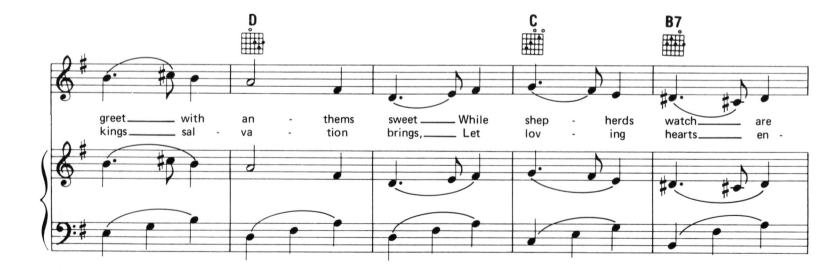

greet_____ with an - thems sweet_____ While shep - herds watch_____ are
kings_____ sal - va - tion brings,_____ Let lov - ing hearts en -

YOU MAKE IT FEEL LIKE CHRISTMAS

Words and Music by
NEIL DIAMOND

YOU'RE ALL I WANT FOR CHRISTMAS

Words and Music by
GLEN MOORE and SEGER ELLIS

Ad lib., dreamily

When Santa comes a-round at Christ-mas time   And

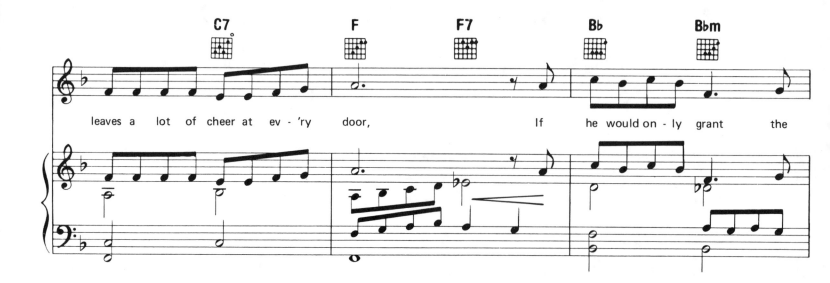

leaves a lot of cheer at ev-'ry door,   If he would on-ly grant the

wish in my heart   I would nev-er ask   for more.

WE WISH YOU A MERRY CHRISTMAS

Brightly

English

We

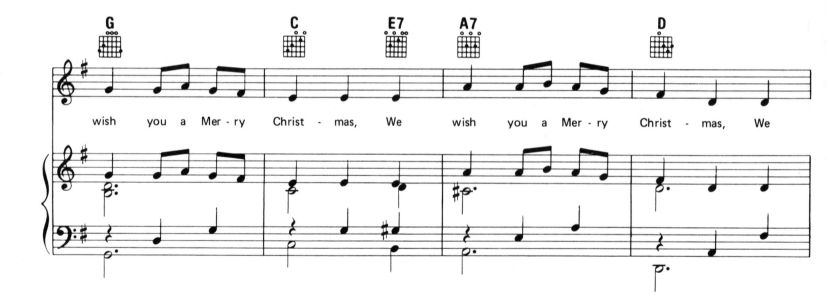

wish you a Mer - ry Christ - mas, We wish you a Mer - ry Christ - mas, We

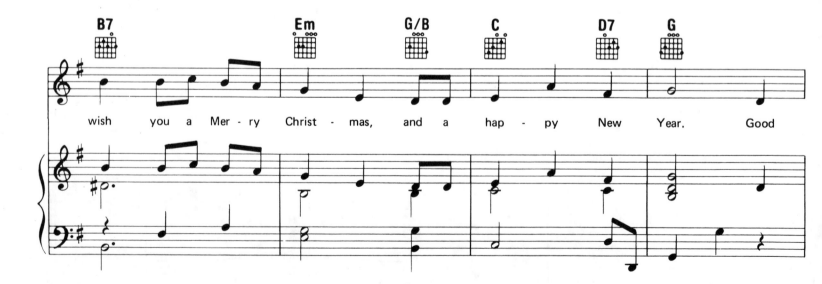

wish you a Mer - ry Christ - mas, and a hap - py New Year. Good

tid - ings we bring to you and your kin, Good

tid - ings for Christ - mas and a hap - py New Year. We

all know that San - ta's com - ing, We all know that San - ta's com - ing, We

all know that San - ta's com - ing, And soon will be here. Good